CO-OPERATIVE PRIDE AND CAPABILITY

The Co-operative Wholesale Society Canning and Preserved Food Factories
Lowestoft

By
Malcolm R. White
2008

GENERAL INFORMATION

Published by Malcolm R. White
Coastal Publications
71 Beeching Drive
Lowestoft
NR32 4TB
First Published June 2008
Copyright © Malcolm R. White 2008

Printed by Micropress Printers Ltd.
27 Norwich Road
Halesworth
Suffolk
IP19 8BX
ISBN 9780954732363
All rights reserved

OTHER TITLES IN THIS UNIQUE SERIES

Please Note - Some of these titles are no longer in print

		ISBN
DOWN THE HARBOUR 1955-1995	40 years of fishing vessels, owners, the harbour and shipyards at Lowestoft	978095324850X
A CENTURY OF FISHING	Fishing from Great Yarmouth and Lowestoft 1899-1999	9780953248518
FISHING WITH DIVERSITY	A portrait of the Colne Group of Lowestoft	9780953248520
CROWNIES OF LOWESTOFT	The steam trawler fleet of Consolidated Fisheries	9780953248537
DRIFTING, TRAWLING & SHIPPING	A portrait of Small & Co. (Lowestoft) Ltd.	9780953248544
THE BOSTON PUTFORD STORY (1)	Fishing and Offshore Support from Great Yarmouth and Lowestoft	9780953248582
HERRINGS, DRIFTERS AND THE PRUNIER TROPHY	Aspects of the vanished herring industry at Yarmouth, Lowestoft and Southwold	9780954732349
THE LOWESTOFT TRAIN	The railway at Lowestoft and scenes on the lines to Norwich, Ipswich and Yarmouth	9780953248568
LOWESTOFT CORPORATION TRANSPORT	Lowestoft Trams, Buses and Bygone Town Scenes	9780953248599
RAILS TO THE COAST	East Anglian Seaside Stations, Sheds and Rail Links-Great Yarmouth and Lowestoft	9780954732301
THE YARMOUTH TRAIN	The railway at Gt. Yarmouth and scenes on the lines to Norwich, Ipswich, Melton Constable and Lowestoft	9780954732325
COACHWORK BY EASTERN COACH WORKS	The East Anglian Bus & Coach Builder	9780954732356
GREETINGS FROM LOWESTOFT	A picture book of old postcards and photographs	9780953248551
LOWESTOFT ANTIQUITY	A picture book of once familiar scenes	9780953248575
A SMILE FROM OLD LOWESTOFT	A celebration of bygone scenes, achievements and features	9780954732332
A DIFFERENT LOWESTOFT	Some missing features of a grand old town	9780954732318

COLOUR KEY :- ———— = MARITIME ———— = TRANSPORT ———— = LOCAL HISTORY

ABOUT THIS BOOK

Every effort has been made to ensure that information contained in this publication is accurate and for this reason numerous sources have been consulted. These include personal accounts of events, official documentation, local diaries, media resources and some accredited research works. However, when considering such a complex historical subject with some details gathered from hand written records that were provided by other parties, 100% accuracy cannot be guaranteed. Books in this series are part of the National Published Archive and as such are included in the library collections of the British Library, the National Library of Scotland, the National Library of Wales, the Universities of Oxford and Cambridge, Trinity College, Dublin and, when appropriate, The National Museum of Science & Industry. This series is published not for financial gain for the author or a commercial publishing house. Any profit that does arise from the sale of books in this series is donated to charity and good causes.

PHOTOGRAPHIC CAPTIONS

Front Cover - A fine view of the former Co-operative Wholesale Society (CWS) factories in December 1995. *(Copyright Mike Page)* **Title Page** - A once familiar scene in Waveney Drive with the No. 1 factory on the right and the No. 2 in the centre of the photograph. *(Copyright Stanley Earl)* **Opposite** - An early finely detailed drawing of the factories and the estate. *(Copyright Co-operative (CWS) Group Ltd./The Malcolm White Collection)*

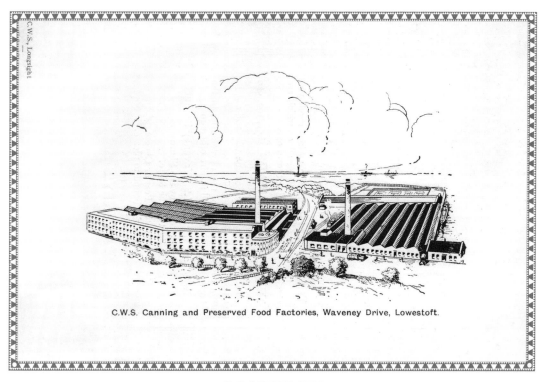

C.W.S. Canning and Preserved Food Factories, Waveney Drive, Lowestoft.

CONTENTS

ACKNOWLEDGEMENTS

I am greatly indebted to Mrs. Florence "Flossie" Baldry, Mrs. Ione Ellis, Mrs. Gwenneth Maclean and Mr. Don Powell for recording and making available their personal recollections of working at the Lowestoft CWS factories. For many years this major food production complex was one of Europe's largest canneries and food processing plants.

By taking time to record their memories, future generations will be made aware of the working conditions, the skills required and the team spirit witnessed whilst working there. The memories of Don, Florence, Gwen and Ione are valuable records of what working at the factories was like and in the future these will be seen as representative of the tasks carried out by thousands of folk who were employed at the factories between 1929 and 1997. In addition to giving readers an interesting and varied insight into the complexities of a large food factory, Don has supplied from his large collection, many of the photographs seen in this publication. I have been very privileged to be able to use these prints which are now irreplaceable and historically very valuable.

For allowing the use of much copyright material originally published by CWS, I am especially grateful to the Co-operative (CWS) Group Ltd. in Manchester.

The cooperation and support offered during the preparation of this book by many kind people interested in recording the industrial heritage of the Lowestoft area is very much appreciated. In addition to those already mentioned, assisting either directly or indirectly in this comprehensive project have been the staff of the Lowestoft Record Office, Mrs. Vivienne Bentley, Mr. Peter Calvert, Mr. Geoff Carefoot, Mrs. Margaret Duckworth, Mr. Stanley Earl, Mr. Norman Fairhead, Mrs. Mabel Haylock, Mr. Peter Killby, Mr. Brian Moses, Mr. Chris Moss/The Dr. Ian Allen Collection, Mr. Michael Page, Mrs. Carol Poole, Mr. Neil Watson and Mrs. Cathryn White. The successful completion of this book, the seventeenth in this unique series, would not have been possible without the valuable help provided by Mr. Stuart Jones BA. Stuart has provided important editorial support for all sixteen titles in the series and has done so again with this latest book.

Sources of information provided by the following have been consulted in the preparation of this book:- 1st East, Barber Richmore, British History-South Millwall (University of London), Business News, Centre for British Film and Television Studies, Chivers Hartley Ltd., Commonwealth War Graves Commission, Corvus Capital, Directory of Trade Names, East of England Development Agency, Eastern Daily Press, English Heritage, Evergreen, Food Trade Review, Government News Network, HM Capital, Hansard, Hicks Muse, Tommy's Pack Fillers, Lion Capital, Hillsdown Holdings plc, Lowestoft Journal, New York Times, Premier Foods Group, Serious Fraud Office, Suffolk County Council, The Competition Commission, The Co-operative Group (CWS) Ltd., The Electronic Telegraph, UK Business Park, Waveney Advertiser and Waveney District Council.
Additional information relating specifically to the history of the CWS has been drawn from the following two CWS publications :-
A Consumers' Democracy - *An account of the origins and growth of the Co-operative Wholesale Society Ltd. and a survey of the structure and its major activities (1951); Co-operative Wholesale Society - The World's Largest Co-operative Trading Organisation (1957).*

PHOTOGRAPHIC OWNERSHIP AND COPYRIGHT

INTRODUCTION

Built adjacent to Lake Lothing with landmark features of high chimneys and substantial buildings occupying a large area of land, the canning and food processing factories in Riverside Road and Waveney Drive dominated the landscape in central Lowestoft until early 2000, when almost all of the buildings and structures of these well known factories were finally cleared away for redevelopment. Only one building remains today that was once part of the CWS Lowestoft estate and this modern style structure is used by a forklift company. No significant reminders of the original factories remain, in fact it is difficult to imagine the factories ever existed.

With a number of relatives who worked at the factories I have a personal interest in recording for all time, the life and times of this bygone local and national asset.

Although generally referred to by townsfolk as the "Co-op", the first and last owner of these food factories was not the Co-operative Wholesale Society or CWS, but Maconochie Bros. until the 1920s, and Premier Foods in the final years. This book focuses on the time when the factories were in the ownership of the CWS, the operator of this substantial industrial complex for the majority of the time that it existed, and a period still fresh in the minds of many folk when the factories were such an important part of Lowestoft life. In 1994, not long after passing into new ownership, the traditional production lines were discontinued leaving two modern food complexes, only completed by the CWS in 1989, in production. These closed in late 1997 bringing an end to food production on the site after over 100 years. In addition to Co-op own label products, in later years the factories produced own label products for Crosse & Blackwell, Quick Thinking and the supermarket giants ASDA, Sainsbury and Tesco.

Over the years the factories were a major financial asset to the area by employing thousands of people and buying vast amounts of local produce for processing and canning thus creating job stability in these supply industries. The services of a great many local firms were required at the factories, and the impact on those businesses was most noticeable as the closures took effect.

The former CWS cannery was the last of the three large local canneries to close, the others being Coastal Canneries and Morton's. During 1953, over 1500 people were employed full time in them, and today with the continued demand for canned products, the work is carried out elsewhere. Following closure, the factories were demolished and the sites cleared, one to make way for a large car dealership and the other for the establishment of a business park that would eventually create hundreds of new jobs for the town. However, at the time of writing (late 2007), the local council and two other partners have decided that instead of the business park, a large civic office complex and marine research establishment will be built on the site with the workforce moving there from existing accommodation.

This publication commemorates the tenth anniversary of the closure of the last part of what was at one time the CWS Lowestoft operation and has been published as a tribute to the thousands of dedicated folk who worked at the factories from the earliest days until the run down and total closure in late 1997. It is designed to be of interest to those who worked there, had relatives that worked there, those generally interested in bygone Lowestoft and in the future, those researching the demise of one of the many, now closed, major industrial concerns in the town.
Hopefully, this book will also impress upon future generations that before council offices and government research facilities existed in Riverside Road, Lowestoft was proud to have one of Europe's largest food production complexes at that location.

Malcolm White
Lowestoft
December 2007

This charming river scene complete with two wherries was used for many applications to promote the wide range of Lowestoft made CWS food products. Dating from the 1930s, it was still to be seen in the 1950s on publicity and advertising literature in co-operative retail stores and elsewhere. Other uses for this portrait of peace and tranquility was on boxes used for transporting goods and on some products. It is assumed that the river is intended to be the Waveney, the brand name given to the larger of the ranges of products made in the town. *(Copyright Co-operative (CWS) Group Ltd./The Malcolm White Collection)*

A Brief History of the Co-operative Wholesale Society

The Co-operative Wholesale Society (CWS) was established in 1863 and can trace its roots back to the mid 1700s, when the first of many small co-operative societies was formed in the north. It was initially known as the North of England Co-operative Wholesale Industrial and Provident Society Ltd.

It was in 1844 that the Rochdale Pioneers Society was established and this led to substantial growth in the co-operative movement. The distribution of a share of the profits, according to the purchases made, to members of the society was one of the eight "Rochdale Rules" laid down by the Rochdale Pioneers. This share of profits became known as the dividend or "divi", and remains a well known feature of purchasing goods and services at co-operative retail outlets today. For a while in the mid 1960s, some co-operative societies issued blue coloured Co-op dividend stamps.

Following the establishment of the CWS, the Co-operative Insurance Society (CIS) was set up in 1867 and the Co-operative Bank in 1872. The Bank was originally the CWS Loan and Deposit Department and became a wholly owned CWS subsidiary in 1971. By the end of 1873 the CWS had started manufacturing, with biscuits being made at Crumpsall in Manchester and shoes at Leicester. The acquisition of their first soap works at Durham in 1874, the first flour mill in 1891 and the first printing works in 1895 were some of the other notable events in the early years of the CWS. Within a short time the CWS was involved in importing, ship owning and the setting up of many overseas ventures. The opening of a depot in New York in 1876 was seen by many as the establishment of the CWS as a world wide buying organisation. In addition to the New York depot, at one time the CWS had depots in Buenos Aires, Denia (Spain), Montreal, Rouen, Sydney, Vancouver, Wellington, and four in Denmark at Aarhus, Copenhagen, Esbjerg and Odense.

Further examples of the rapid expansion of the CWS are that by 1921, the CWS owned over 34,000 acres of land in the United Kingdom, and during 1920 started a cattle market at Gisburn, a butter factory in Carlisle, and also a fish processing depot at Fleetwood. After World War One, the English and Scottish Wholesale Societies became substantial owners of tea Estate Farms when they purchased approximately 32,000 acres of tea plantations in India and Ceylon (now Sri Lanka). In 1921, the CWS opened a large depot in West Africa and started purchasing palm kernels direct from the local inhabitants for shipping to their oil mills in Liverpool. Part of the mill output went direct to the CWS soap and candle factory at Irlam.

The number of co-operative societies continued to increase and by 1900, there were 1439. By 1914, this number had reduced to 1,385 due to the amalgamation of some of the societies. Today this process of creating fewer but much larger co-operative societies continues and at the beginning of the 21st century, the number of societies had fallen to 45.

The years following World War One saw the establishment of the Co-operative Party which was intended to give the movement a voice in both Parliamentary and local government, and the Co-operative College in Manchester. By this time, the number of CWS factories and production units producing a vast range of food and non food products had grown enormously. During 1934, a retail division was set up to develop areas of the country where co-operative societies did not exist or where the local society was struggling. A ten year plan was formulated in 1935 that encouraged existing co-operatives to expand into areas not served by co-ops and were adjacent to their existing sales area. In 1957, this division became the Co-operative Retail Services (CRS).

During World War Two the first self service shop was opened by the London Co-operative Society in 1942. Further growth in the retail co-operative presence on the High Street occurred in 1945 with the establishment of the National Co-operative Chemists (NCC). The NCC was the first national chain of retail shops co-operatively owned in Britain and now has 800 branches including 50 in Scotland.

In the 21st century, the products originating or derived from the Co-operative (CWS) Group's own sources are limited, but in the past the range of goods and services was enormous and just about everything needed for the home could be supplied by the CWS.

For a great many years, daily needs such as bread, milk and coal were delivered to most households in the British Isles by the local retail Co-operative society's baker, milkman or coalman with the commodities generally originating from the CWS. In the case of coal, the CWS had a fleet of coal trucks to bring bulk coal from the colliery to local depots via the railway. Similarly, CWS tankers transported bulk milk on the railway from the country to the town and city for processing and bottling.

The following list from 1950 gives an idea of the scope and range of the activities of the Society. It contains factories, cotton, woollen and flour mills, works, production units and estate farms in the UK, and the goods and work they produced, processed or carried out. Not all of these were in production during the same period.

Accrington	Cotton Weaving
Acton	Preserves and Pickles
Ardsley	Wagon Building
Ashwellthorpe	Seed Testing
Avonmouth	Flour Mills
Barnsley	Preserves
Batley	Wool Weaving
Bedford	Footwear and Canisters
Beeston	Hides and Skins
Birkenhead	Slumberware
Birmingham	Aluminium Ware, Bedsteads, Furniture, Cycles and Motorcycles, Prams, Scales, Wagons
Birtley	Canisters, Dairy Equipment, Tinware
Bolton-on-Dearne	Hosiery
Bradford	Spinning and Wool Weaving
Bridgewater	Aerated Waters
Brislington	Aerated Waters, Butter, Cheese, Men's Wear
Bristol	Bedding, Furniture, Motor Bodies, Scales, Upholstery
Broughton	Bedding, Clothing, Cotton Weaving, Furniture, Mantles, Men's Wear, Shirts
Buckfastleigh	Fellmongering, Rugs, Wool Combing
Bury	Cotton Weaving
Cardiff	Biscuits, Butter, Cheese, Meat

	Preparations, Motor Bodies, Scales, Shirts
Chesterfield	Aerated Waters
Clayton	Vinegar, Yeast
Clitheroe	Estate Farm
Cockburn Hatley	Estate Fruit Farm
Coldham	Estate Farm
Crewe	Men's Clothing, Estate Farm
Cricklewood	Biscuits
Crumpsall	Biscuits, Confectionary
Darlington	Glasshouses
Derby	Seed Testing, Paints, Scales, Footwear
Durham	Seed Testing
Denton	Hats
Dob Cross	Shirting's, Woollens
Down Ampney	Dairy, Estate Farm
Droylesdon	Biscuits, Confectionary, Drug Works
Dudley	Buckets, Electrical Fittings, Fenders, Holloware, Steel Equipment, Sweepers, Washing Machines
Dunstan	Flour, Soap
Enderby	Footwear
Enfield	Cabinets, Furniture
Exeter	Aerated Waters
Fleetwood	Fish
Goole	Estate Farm
Grappenhall	Tanneries
Grimsby	Fish
Guide Bridge	Wagon Building and Repairing
Hebden Bridge	Fustian, Cotton Weaving, Men's Wear
Heckmondwike	Footwear
Heswall	Frocks and Overalls
Hetton and Holborn	Estate Farms
Higher Irlam	Margarine, Suet
Hull	Flour, Scales, Bacon
Huthwaite	Hosiery
Ipswich	Scales
Irlam	Candles, Detergents, Soap, Margarine
Keighley	Bedsteads, Bicycle and Piano Parts,
(Ironworks)	General Ironwork, Washing and

	Wringing Machines (Mangles), Wire Mattresses
Kempston	Footwear
Kenner Valley	Glass Houses
Kettering	Corsets
Knottingley	Pottery
Lea Bridge	Ladies Clothing
Leeds	Butter, Brushes, Footwear, Hides and Skins, Mantles, Men's Wear, Mats, Scales
Leek	Knitted Wear
Leicester	Box Making, Footwear, Paint, Printing, Wagons
Leyton	Footwear, Blouses, Underclothing, Frocks, Skirts
Littleborough	Blankets, Flannel
Liverpool	Cattle Food, Scales, Seed Crushing, Dog Biscuits, Rusks, Oil and Cake Mills, Provender, Wheat buying
Llanrwst	Aerated Waters and cordials, Creamery
London	Building, Butter, Coffee, Engineering, Food Packing, Furs, Meat, Men's Wear, Optical Scales, Tea, Warehousing
Long Eaton	Bedding, Furniture, Upholstery
Longsight	Printing and Bookbinding
Longton	Bone China, Earthenware, Tiles
Lowestoft	Canned and Preserved Foods, Quick Freezing
Luton	Cocoa and Chocolate
Manchester	Abattoirs, Bedding, Building, Cartwrighting, Casemaking, Engineering, Clothing, Flour, Food Packing, Framing, Frocks, Furniture, Hats and Caps, Hides and Skins, Kiddies Outwear, Men's Clothing, Motor Body Workshop, Optical Workshop, Pest Destruction, Printing, Provender, Sawmills, Shop Fitting, Tea and Coffee, Ties, Tobacco and Cigars, Umbrellas, Underclothing, Vinegar

	and Yeast, Weighing Machines
Marden	Estate Fruit Farm
Middleton Junction	Aerated Waters, Pickles, Sauces, Motor Bodies, Scales, Picture Framing
Newcastle-upon-Tyne	Building, Cartwrighting, Engineering, Hides and Skins, Leather Goods, Picture Framing
North Shields	Fish
Northampton	Butter, Footwear, Fellmongering, Footwear
Norwich	
Nottingham	Aerated Waters, Cordials, Scales
Oldham	Flour Mill
Patricroft	Rope and Twine
Pelaw	Bedding, Clothing, Drysaltery, Furniture, Leather Goods and Saddlery, Packing, Polishes, Preserves, Printing, Quilts, Scales, Shirts, Vinegar
Pendleton	Glass Bottles and Jars
Peterborough	Wagon Building and Repair
Plymouth	Bedding, Furniture, Scales, Upholstery
Pontefact	Glue and Size, Fellmongering
Portsmouth	Mantles
Preston	Footwear
Radcliffe	Cotton Weaving, Furniture
Rawtenstall	Footwear
Reading	Mantles, Pickles and Sauces, Preserves, Vinegar, Printing
Reddish	Confectionery, Printing
Rixton	Estate Farm
Rochdale	Paints, Varnishes
Roden	Glasshouses, Estate Farm
Rotherham	Pottery
Rushden	Footwear
Salford	Saw Mill
Sheffield	Cutlery, Garden Tools, Jackets and Overalls, Scales, Shirts
Shepton Mallet	Bacon, Meat Preparations
Shilbottle	Colliery
Silvertown	Flour, Soap, Sweets, Cordials
Skelmersdale	Cotton Weaving
Slaithwaite	Provender

Southampton	Scales
Sowerby Bridge	Flour
St. Helens	Gloves
Stockton	Preserves, Scales
Stoughton	Estate Farm
Street	Tanneries
Trafford Park	Bacon, Packing
Treforest	Aerated Waters, Bedding, Furniture
Upminster	Shirts, Dairy Equipment
Warburton	Estate Farm
Warrington	Cardboard Boxes and Printing
Wellingborough	Footwear, Corsets
West Hartlepool	Lard
Westborough	Corsets
Winsford	Bacon, Meat Preparations
Withgill	Estate Farm and Meat Products
Woking	Motor Body Building
Workington	Aerated Waters
Worksop	Glass Bottles
Wymondham	Brushes and Mats

Other Depots and Salerooms

The C.W.S. had Depots and Salerooms at Manchester, Newcastle, Bristol, Liverpool, Nottingham, Huddersfield, London, Cardiff, Northampton, Plymouth, Leeds and Birmingham. The Traffic Departments were at Manchester, London, Newcastle, Bristol and Northampton.

Other Dairies and establishments

There were also Dairies at the following places:- Basford Bridge (near Crewe), Carlisle, Chaigley (Lancashire), Clapham Junction (London), Congleton (Cheshire), Cricklade (Wiltshire), Etchingham (Sussex), Fairfach (South Wales), Fole (Uttoxeter), Lianharan (Glamorgan), Melksham (Wiltshire), Penrhyn (Merionethshire), Somerby (Leicestershire), Stowmarket (Suffolk), Wallingford (Berkshire), Witham (Essex) and Poultry Farming at Mitton, near Stonyhurst (Lancashire), and Farming and Piggeries at Withgill, also near Stonyhurst.

Many other important CWS owned production centres and depots existed abroad, including coffee estates, bacon factories in Denmark and Ireland, and meat freezing plants in New Zealand.

The following brief histories and activities of a **small selection** of CWS establishments in the early 1900s provide an interesting insight into the wide range of goods and services at one time provided by the Society.

Avonmouth - CWS Flour Mills
Opened in 1910 and standing beside a deep dock, this mill was designed to allow discharge from ships laden with wheat directly into the mill silos. Within 5 years of opening the capacity of the mill had been doubled.

Bury - CWS Weaving Shed
All kinds of materials were produced by the weavers on the 900 looms. Complete with the latest machinery, the Weaving Shed opened in 1905 and was described as "up to date in every respect with an ample volume of light and the floor space gives plenty of room for every branch of the work".

Desborough - CWS Corset Factory
CWS corset making commenced in 1898 at Manchester and within a few years the factory building was unable to cope with the demand and a new one was constructed at Desborough. It was claimed that the products from the factory were unequalled in style or comfort and should be found in every drapery store.

Huthwaite - CWS Hosiery Factory
This factory was erected about fourteen miles from Nottingham in 1908 and produced all kinds of hosiery such as stockings, socks, together with underclothing and cardigans. The factory prided itself in producing the finest hosiery products available.

Keighley - CWS Iron Works
The works were acquired in 1908 and within a short time were considerably altered and enlarged. In the early years the principal articles of manufacture were washing machines and wringers, bicycle and piano frame parts, iron and brass bedsteads and wire mattresses. Miscellaneous ironwork requirements could also be produced at Keighley.

London - CWS Leman Street Branch
This branch was established in 1874 on very modest lines to cater for the co-operative societies in the south of England and within a

short time saw rapid expansion. Major enlargement of the branch was necessary, and in 1887 a new large building complete with an impressive clock tower was erected. Further expansion took place in 1910 when a new wing was added to accommodate the drapery department.

London - CWS Tea Department
In 1882, the CWS and Scottish Wholesale Society (SCWS) federated to establish the Tea Department. This large factory was described at the time as "splendidly equipped with numerous labour saving appliances and has the latest inventions in weighting and packing machinery installed". Annual sales of tea in the years leading up to World War One were typically 38,000,000lbs. per year. For many years the Societies owned extensive tea plantations in India and Ceylon (now Sri Lanka).

Luton - CWS Cocoa Works
Opening in 1902, this works was run jointly by the CWS and the SCWS. The building was described as a light spacious factory equipped with the best machinery available for making fine cocoas equal to any other British or Foreign make.

Manchester - CWS Central Premises
The CWS began business in a small office at Manchester in 1864. The first complete year's sales were £120,000 and by 1915 this had reached £43,000,000 when the number of employees was 27,000. A group of substantial and impressive buildings were erected in Manchester to cope with the major growth in the co-operative movement throughout the country.

Manchester - CWS Printing Works
These works were located at Longsight and were described thus, "the whole of the allied trades connected with the printing business are engaged in these works - printing, binding, ruling, lithographing, bag making, box construction and illustrating". It was claimed that these works, employing 1400 people, were the finest in the country.

Manchester - CWS Sun Flour Mill
This mill was purchased in 1906 when the output of milled products was 35 sacks per hour. Following enlargement of the buildings and the installation of more modern machinery by the CWS

the output had been increased to 150 sacks per hour by World War One. This large property was on the banks of the Manchester Ship Canal and with large railway sidings adjacent was considered to be in a most advantages position.

Manchester - CWS Tobacco Factory
The trade in tobacco goods was considerable in the mid 1890s and the CWS acquired a small factory in 1898 to enable it to embark on the manufacture of tobacco products. The demand for CWS brand products was substantial and within a few years the floor area had been extended to 30,000 square feet. In the 1920s, the annual factory production was typically 1,500 tons of tobacco, 4,440,000 cigars and 81,000,000 cigarettes.

Middleton Junction - CWS Jam, Pickle and Vinegar Works
Prior to World War One, at least 15,000 tons of jam and marmalade were produced annually besides huge quantities of candied peel and mincemeat. Much of the vast amount of fruit used in the Works came from CWS owned Estate Farms.

Newcastle-on-Tyne - CWS West Blandford Street Premises
The branch was established in 1871 and "with a rapidity characteristic of the institution, the trade rapidly outgrew the accommodation". Acquired premises were extended and many buildings were erected in the vicinity of West Blandford Street including a fine majestic office building with several workshops and warehouses to cater for the trades that Newcastle was renowned for.

Rochdale - CWS Paint, Colour and Varnish Works
These substantial premises were opened in November 1911 and were equipped for the manufacture of tinned paints to supply the household, painting and building departments of Co-operative Societies shops. The works also produced special paints, varnishes and distempers for the many requirements of the CWS works and building departments.

Silvertown - CWS Flour Mill
Erected in 1898, this mill was built to cope with the demand from the southern societies for milled products. The mill was on the banks of the River Thames and had a direct railway link into it. Initially the capacity of the mill machinery was 12 sacks weighing 280lbs each hour, but by 1915 the output was 50 sacks per hour.

CWS logos of the 1950s.
(Copyright Co-operative (CWS) Group Ltd. / The Malcolm White Collection)

In the 1950s, the combined membership of the many Co-operative Societies was approximately 11¾ millions, and the CWS operated over 200 productive establishments. There were 31,000 retail shops and other outlets of which approximately 24,000 were food shops of one type or another with the remainder supplying household goods, clothing and furniture. Market penetration was 20% for food, and around 12% for non food. Within a few years a new chain of non food retails shops was set up to sell footwear; this chain became Shoefayre in 1964. The processing of milk was one important aspect of the CWS, and in 1957 their 34 creameries handled no less than 157,263,000 gallons of milk. An indication of the wide range of CWS products at this time was the manufacturing of television and radio sets under the "Defiant" brand, pianos under the "Amyl" brand and electric light bulbs and tubes under the "Luma" brand.

The year 1966 saw the revision of Co-operative movement principles by the International Co-operative Alliance. One outcome of this was the amalgamation of the then 680 local societies into 55 larger regional societies being called for. A new national "Co-op" logo was launched in 1968 as part of a project designed to give the movement a new image.
During 1973, the SCWS which had been formed in 1868, merged with the CWS. This led to the CWS becoming directly involved in retailing. Calls for further consolidation within the Co-operative retail movement were made with the launching of a regional plan that contained proposals for amalgamation of the then 260 societies into 26 large regional societies. In line with the much discussed policy of consolidation, the large London Co-operative Society transferred to the Co-operative Retail Services (CRS) in 1981, the Royal Arsenal Co-operative Society

transferred to the CWS in 1985 followed by the North Eastern Co-operative Society in 1990. Some other developments during the 1980s and 1990s included the CWS, Britain's largest Estate Farmer, banning hunting with hounds on their farmland, the Co-operative Congress proposing to reduce the number of societies to 25 and the Co-operative movement placing a ban on South African goods, although this was lifted in 1992.

A major change in the Co-operative movement's food manufacturing capability occurred in 1994 when Hobson plc purchased F. E. Barber Ltd., a CWS subsidiary for in excess of £100 million. The sale comprised a number of factories that provided the CWS with its own brand products that were sold throughout the Co-op chain of around 800 nationwide retail stores. Hobson plc subsequently sold off the packing, canning and oils and fats divisions. At the time that F.E. Barber Ltd. was acquired, Hobson plc negotiated a deal with the CWS to supply them with own label products for 3 years until November 1999. In 1995, the CWS agreed an extension of a further 2½ years to the original 3 year supply contract. Soon after this contract was agreed Hobson plc were themselves sold to Hillsdown Holdings plc for £121 million. The Chief Executive of Hobson plc at that time was Mr. Andrew Regan, who in 1997 led an attempt to gain control of the CWS in a £1.2 billion takeover bid which was repelled by the membership. The result of the takeover of Hobson plc was that F. E. Barber Ltd. and the former CWS Lowestoft operation became a subsidiary of Hillsdown Holdings plc.

Smile, one of the first on line internet based banks was set up by the Co-operative Bank in 1999 and during 2000, the CWS and CRS merged. The following year the CWS changed its identity to the Co-operative Group (CWS) Ltd.

During 2002 the Co-operative Group (CWS) Ltd. acquired 600 Allday stores, the Yorkshire Co-operative and United Co-operative merged, and the Co-operative Bank combined with Co-operative Insurance (CIS) to form Co-operative Financial Services (CFS). During 2003 the Balfour chain of 76 convenience stores and newsagents were acquired and the Co-operative Travel Trading Group was launched.

An important announcement was made at the end of 2006

concerning a merger between the Co-operative Group and United Co-operatives (United Co-op). The United Co-op operated across Yorkshire, the North West and north Midlands and was considered the largest regional consumer co-operative in the United Kingdom. United Co-operatives was set up as the result of the merger of United NorWest, Yorkshire, Sheffield and Leeds co-operatives. The amalgamation of the Co-operative Group and United Co-operatives took place in July 2007.

Figures released by the Co-operative Group show that they operate over 4,500 trading establishments including 1713 supermarkets and community food outlets, 372 pharmacies, 609 funeral directors, 358 travel agents, 283 shoe retailers, estate farms (70,000 acres in England and Scotland), electrical retail outlets, filling stations and garages, hotels, financial services, furniture retail outlets, insurance and internet banking.

The Group is responsible for some 4,500 food and non-food products, marketed under the Co-operative brand label and supplied to retail societies. Co-operative Group estate farms grow a variety of cereals which go into Co-operative flour and a range of fruit and vegetables that go into Co-operative stores. A new venture for the Group is investing in the renewable energy market by building wind turbines for power generation on estate farmland it owns. The Co-operative Group (CWS) Ltd. is the world's largest consumer co-operative with a turnover of more than £9 billion, has 4.5 million members and 87,500 employees. The intention is that all parts of the Group will operate under a uniform brand - The Co-operative, although this has not yet (late 2007) been fully adopted in some parts of the UK.

In 2007, Her Majesty the Queen graciously conferred the Queen's Award to the Co-operative Group (CWS) Ltd. in recognition of their outstanding achievements in "Approach to Sustainable Development".

Within the co-operative movement there are many co-operative societies including consumer Co-ops such as Anglia Regional Co-operative Society and East of England Co-operative Society. There are also Agricultural Co-ops, Co-op Publications, the Phone Co-op, Worker Co-ops and many others.

It was often stated that there was little that the CWS did not make or provide for their members. In 2007, the CWS launched an advertising campaign promoting food items grown on their own estate farms. This raised awareness that many of the greengrocery items sold in Co-operative Shops are actually produced by the CWS and not purchased from outside suppliers as with other food retailers.

THE CWS AT LOWESTOFT

During the early 1870s, James and Archibald White Maconochie settled in Lowestoft and established a business in the Belvedere Road area; this was followed later by another in Raglan Street. Their early products included preserved provisions such as pickled onions and processed mackerel, herring and sardines. At one time James lived in the High Street and Archibald at Boston Lodge in Church Road. With expansion in mind, in 1890 the brothers purchased a large area of land on the south bank of Lake Lothing and after building the adjacent roadway, established a factory there for producing canned and preserved food products. James died in February 1895 and was buried in Lowestoft Cemetery close to the chapel. His grave is marked by an elegant obelisk complete with bronze plaque showing his profile. Other members of the Maconochie family are buried in the same plot. The Company retained Maconochie Bros. as their trading name following the death of James.

A large unique commemoration stone inscribed with a message noting the Maconochie Bros. association with the area was a well known feature of the now demolished No. I factory boundary wall in Waveney Drive for almost 100 years. Like many other aspects of historic Lowestoft, the wall, stone and factories were swept away to make way for numerous redevelopment projects. A preserved small section of the original wall together with the

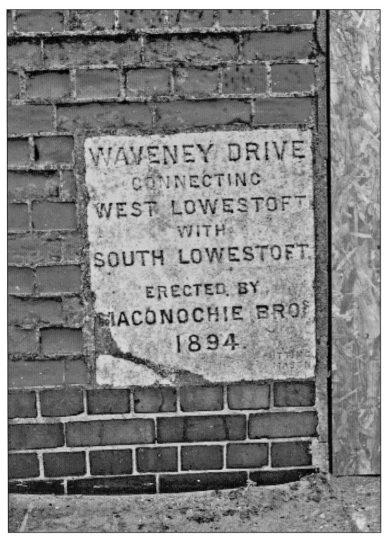

This stone commemorated the extensive development of south Lowestoft by the Maconochie Bros. It was a valued feature of the boundary wall facing Waveney Drive at the No. I factory for over 100 years. This historically valuable stone disappeared during the regeneration of the site and at the time of writing (late 2007) has not reappeared. *(Copyright Stuart Jones)*

stone would have been a superb reminder to future generations of the major food factories that once fed millions of people in this country and overseas.

Maconochie Bros. were wholesale provision merchants and manufacturers of pickles, potted meat and fish, jam, marmalade and other preserved foods with a head office and factory in London and also businesses nationwide including at Fraserburgh, Hadfield, Hull, Millwall, and Stornoway. The factory at Fraserburgh, which opened in 1883 and closed in 1953, had a long association with the herring fishing industry and was well known to Lowestoft and Yarmouth fishermen whilst fishing from the north eastern Scottish ports. Interestingly a building at one time part of the Maconochie Bros. premises at Hull, has been retained and is now Grade II listed.

By the early 1900s, in addition to a large home market, Maconochie Bros. were exporting substantial quantities of their products abroad and during World War One, as contractors to the Admiralty and War Office, produced tens of thousands of tinned products for the armed forces. One of the best known of these was the Army Ration Beef and Vegetable stew. Described in the firm's advertising material as "a ready cooked delicious stew served in 20 minutes", it was also available to the general public at 1/6d a can. Other products known to have produced included cans of Pork and Beans, Vegetables and Pickles, one variety of which was Red Cabbage. It is not possible to ascertain whether any of these products were produced at the Lowestoft cannery, but it is highly likely that they were. In addition to the Army Rations, a very well known product made by the company was "Pan Yan" pickle, which was first made around 1907 at their London factory. This product is apparently no longer (2007) marketed by the successors to Maconochie Bros. although a relaunch of the product is possible.

In London, Maconochie Bros. built a new pickle factory, a jam, peel and candy factory, vegetable kitchens, riverside warehouses, stores, workshops, a large cooperage and offices. At Lowestoft the firm continued to expand and plans were drawn up during 1915 for a second factory to be constructed immediately west of their first factory.

According to the Metropolitan Borough of Poplar records, Archibald, at one time a Liberal Unionist MP, died in February 1926. Within a few years both Lowestoft factories passed into the ownership of the Co-operative Wholesale Society (CWS). According to Co-operative Group sources, the negotiations for the purchase of the Maconochie Estate at Lowestoft extended from 1927 until 1932, by which time the deals for the two factories were finally completed. The CWS was in occupation of the older factory by the autumn of 1929, having previously operated a fish processing plant at Great Yarmouth. The official opening of the second factory was in September 1933 with the total CWS Lowestoft site by then being around 13.5 acres. The Great Co-operative Exhibition was held in Lowestoft that year to mark the opening of the second factory.

Although completed by Maconochie Bros., it is understood that due to a disagreement with the Corporation, they never occupied the new three storey second factory. This building, that became the CWS No. 2 factory, was equipped with goods lifts for easy access between floors and had lift rooms on the roof with the letter "C" on one, "W" on the next and "S" on the other. It had a large cellar that during World War Two was used by management, staff and employees as an air raid shelter during attacks by enemy aircraft on the town.

The CWS expanded production lines considerably and by the late 1930s the Lowestoft factories were producing a wide range of "Waveney ", "Unity" and "Wheatsheaf " branded lines that included cheese and meat products, a range of soups, bakery products, pies, puddings, canned fish and vegetables including peas, butter beans and carrots. A very special product for which the CWS at Lowestoft became famous was "Jennie" brand herrings in tomato sauce. In 1930, a film was made that followed the complete process of canning the herring and included such detail as putting the "Jennie" label on the finished product by hand, prior to it being packed and dispatched to the shops.

During 1932 plans were made to extend the general office and a new warehouse and loading bay were constructed. In addition to vast quantities of raw materials arriving by rail, at this time much of the output of the factories left by the railway with trains leaving the private sidings for a variety of destinations. Until late in the life of the No. 2 factory, the railway was used to deliver fuel for the oil fired boilers, with the rail tankers being shunted down the siding next to Riverside Road.

In World War One, what became the CWS No. 1 factory produced vast quantities of tinned and packaged food for the armed forces and during World War Two, both factories were given special priority by the Government due to the essential war work carried out there. The factories and the area around them became the subject of many air attacks during World War Two. An example of this was that in 1940 over 100 bombs were dropped on the town by enemy aircraft. At the factories, the employees frequently disappeared into the air raid shelter causing a stoppage of work.

In June 1949, a Roll of Honour was made and erected by the CWS (Lowestoft) Factories Employees Sports Association in memory of nine people who were either killed in action, died whilst on military service or who were killed by enemy air action over Lowestoft and had worked at the factories. During November 1995, this fine memorial and a statuette were given to local museums for safe keeping and display. The statuette was officially known as the "Mary Cottrell Trophy" but unofficially as the "Jennie Trophy". It was first used as a trophy in 1935 at the annual sports event. A happy and contented workforce is the key to the success of any business and to this effect singing on the Lowestoft production lines was allowed and helped pass the time away whilst working on what some may have considered boring and uninteresting work.

The late 1940s saw the Lowestoft factories venture into a new line in food production when they expanded into quick freezing of fruit and vegetables. In 1950, the tens of thousands of cans, glass bottles and jars used in the factories arrived by rail from the CWS factories at Bedford and Worksop, previously the tin containers were made in the factory at Lowestoft. In later years both glass containers and cans were supplied by outside suppliers. An impressive output valued at over £1,200,000 was achieved in 1950 by Lowestoft CWS when the full time workforce numbered 520. In addition to the full time staff, casual labour was employed to help cope with seasonal products such as herring and peas, thereby increasing the total number of employees considerably.

The publicity film "Peas" was made by the CWS Film Unit at the Lowestoft factories in 1951; this featured the mechanical harvesting and canning of peas. The film comprehensively covered the complete canning process and followed the peas from the field to being shelled, cleaned, washed, blanched, graded with unwanted peas being removed by hand, and then being canned, cooked and labelled. Laboratory testing was shown being carried out at every stage of production. The fact that at Lowestoft, peas went from the field to being canned in 2½ hours was emphasised during the film.

A wide range of products continued to be made at Lowestoft in the 1950s including canned vegetables, baked beans, canned fish, processed cheese, soups, cooked meats, meat pastes, fish paste, meat pies, sausages and potato crisps.

The factories were always in demand by visitors who wished to see around this vast food processing operation and witness the production stages of the various lines making the products that Lowestoft was renowned for. In order to make tours of the factories as professional as possible, a group of very knowledgeable ladies who excelled in dealing with customers were asked to act as guides. This was in addition to the normal work within the factories that they undertook. Typical visitors were the group of officials from the Rugby Co-operative Society on 29th- 30th May 1934, and 25 officials and Grocery Branch managers of the Keighley Industrial Co-operative Society in Yorkshire, who visited the factories in November 1955. It was usual on these occasions for the visit to be commemorated with a formal group portrait that included local CWS officials on completion of the visit. Traditionally visitors to the factories came from far and wide, another example being on 20th April 1938 when the Frankfurt City Schools Football Team visited the factories as part of a programme of high profile events organised by town leaders during their 10 day stay in Lowestoft. The German lads played various local football teams and their stay also included visits to the Broads, Bury St Edmunds, Gt. Yarmouth, London, Norwich, Somerleyton Hall and the residence of Brigadier-General Sir Thomas Jackson, Bart., DSO, MVO, JP.

Made in 1961, "It's in the Can" was another CWS film shot at Lowestoft. This included many scenes in and around the factories where employees were seen at work. It featured various stages of the production of many products made at the factories. At least two further CWS films were made locally, one of which featured the factories. These films illustrated lesser known aspects of the co-operative movement and the many activities it was involved in. During 1938 the film "Rogerson Hall" was completed, this demonstrated the facilities of Rogerson Hall, a CWS/Workers Travel

For over 70 years the No. 2 factory chimney was a familiar sight from all over Lowestoft. A new lightning conductor was fitted in May 1989 and just visible in this view are two steeplejacks working at the top of the structure, one dressed in blue is in the centre, and the other is on the left side. At that time the chimney contained individual liners for each of the three Robey factory boilers. *(Copyright Don Powell)*

Association run holiday camp which was situated mid way between Corton and Hopton. The facilities included the 239ft. beach at the front of the camp, lounges, writing rooms, chalets, the fine gardens complete with fountains, kitchens, dining rooms, table tennis room and outside badminton courts and the children's playground. The camp was well situated with regular local and long distance trains serving the nearby railway stations at Corton and Hopton. The main building still exists today but most of the 1938 features shown in the film have disappeared or have been drastically changed with caravans and mobile homes very much in evidence in 2007. The hall was named after Cecil Rogerson, the secretary of the Workers Travel Association. The other film was called "Pathfinders Camp" and featured the Kessingland Youth Camp which was held in August 1951. The camp was operated by the Holiday Fellowship with much of the organisation by the Co-operative Youth Movement. The film was made with assistance from the Gravesend, Royal Arsenal and Grays Co-operative Societies and featured camp scenes, rambles, sports day and a visit to the CWS factories at Lowestoft.

By the 1970s, the factories were in desperate need of new investment and replacement of some of the older plant. The CWS responded by spending a vast sum of money on new lines, plant and equipment. As well as supplying the Co-operative sector, the Lowestoft factories supplied many food retailers and wholesalers through a subsidiary company. In a 1981 press statement, the then factory manager Mr. Peter Loman stated that for some time the Lowestoft factories had been threatened with closure together with hundreds of job losses since they were unprofitable. However the 1980 financial results for Lowestoft were the best for four years and he went on to say "we have had a more profitable year than we have had for a long time and in an industry which has suffered declining profit margins, it is a pleasing result".

In the late 1980s and early 1990s, the CWS spent over £15 million installing new production lines and facilities at Lowestoft. This investment concerned the installation of high speed cookers, a ready meal complex and a bottling plant for sauces and pickles. Already one of the largest canneries in Europe, the new investment enabled the factories to supply a wider range of products that included a new line of 12 ambient temperature ready meals to Co-op stores and own label customers. The Minister of Agriculture, Fisheries and Food, the Rt. Hon. John Selwyn Gummer

Moving of bulky items was an ongoing requirement at the factories. In the No. 2 long store warehouse, Peter Harvey is busy using a fork lift to move boxes of cans.
(Courtesy Peter Calvert)

MP, opened the first purpose built production centre for ready meals in September 1989. Unlike chilled or frozen meals these new products could be held at ambient temperatures for up to a year with no deterioration and included Lasangne, Chilli Con Carne, Moussaka, Beef Rogan Josh and Pasta Bolognese. Other items manufactured on the new lines included ketchup, salad cream dressing and sweet pickle. Mr. Gummer's visit to Lowestoft came at a time when the factories were the subject of a major development and modernisation programme which seemed to indicate a secure future for the CWS operation in the town and importantly, hundreds of jobs.

At one time the CWS was a major employer with up to 900 employees in the summer and about 750 during the rest of the year and like other bygone major local industries made a very substantial financial input to the local economy. It was with deep regret that the Society had to announce 29 job losses in September 1990 due to streamlining of the work processes. In September 1992, when the operations manager was Mr. Dennis Bean, the factories featured the very latest plant and machinery with computerised processes dealing with canned goods ranging from fresh vegetables, puddings and baked beans to the extensive range of ready meals and sauces already mentioned. At this time 55% of the Lowestoft factories output was sold to companies other than the Co-operative movement and the production levels were running at 250 million cans of food, 50 million glass containers of food and 2½ million ready meals per year. This was a superb performance from one of Europe's largest food producing units and an achievement that Lowestoft could be proud of.

Throughout the life of the CWS at Lowestoft, industrial relations were generally good and an excellent sports and social club existed with fine facilities provided for members. Occasions such as the CWS (Lowestoft) Employees Sports Association-Badminton Section winning the Lowestoft & District Badminton League for the 1950-51 season, was just one event when sporting representatives from the factories workforce featured in the pages of the local newspaper.

Another well known and much respected aspect of the social and recreational life of the factories was the very active group of employees who frequently staged variety shows and concert parties on the stage of the Riverside Road staff dining room. Plays such as "The Ghost Train", complete with train noises, and shows such as "The Black and White Minstrels" and "Snow White and the Seven Dwarfs" were typical examples of the entertainment provided by talented members of the Lowestoft CWS workforce. Regular performers on the stage over the years included Joe Barret, Johnnie Cleveland, George Ellis, Eddie Jessop, Johnnie Orton and Joe Sharman. Occasional appearances by professional performers and actors such as John Stuart were also arranged. The stage shows helped create a family atmosphere in the factories and produce a workforce that was content, happy and hard working. The CWS stage shows continued well into the 1960s.

The CWS at Lowestoft was in the news in 1989 and again in 1992 for an unexpected reason. The long running local saga of a new southern relief road and a new road crossing of Lake Lothing produced in December 1989 a Government paper favouring an option that would have a mid harbour crossing in the vicinity of the Co-operative Wholesale Society factories. The road would connect with the proposed South Lowestoft relief road and the northern spine road. The Society was not in agreement with this and presented alternative proposals for the relief road and harbour crossing. In July 1992, the local Conservative MP Mr. David Porter raised the issue with the Secretary of State and requested information about what had happened to the CWS proposals. The reply was that they were the subjects of a detailed economic, environmental and engineering assessment and that was expected to be completed in August or September.

A notable event occurred on 6th December 1991 when the CWS at Lowestoft received a Quality Assurance Award from the British Standards Institute. The framed "BSI Registered Firm" certificate was presented by Mr. David Porter MP, and applied to quality assurance in "canning, snack foods and ready meals". At that time the future of the factories under CWS ownership seemed secure. However, major changes were on the way for the Lowestoft CWS operation and the workforce.

During the 1990s, F. E. Barber Ltd. was the name under which the Lowestoft factories operated and in May 1994, Hobson plc purchased F. E. Barber Ltd. from the Co-operative Wholesale Society and subsequently decided to sell off the packing, cannery, oils and fats divisions.

On the 14th October 1994, it was announced at short notice by

Demolition at the rear of the No. 2 factory in February 2000 as seen from Waveney Drive. The removal from the landscape of such an imposing building was decided after further use was planned for the location and finance became available in April 1999 from the East of England Development Agency.
The £3.6 million regeneration project for the Business Park included £685,000 from the European Objective 5B scheme.
(Copyright Don Powell)

Hobson plc to a meeting of all the Lowestoft employees in the factory canteen that the great majority of the Lowestoft operation would close with the loss of 350 jobs. It was reported that the employees would be given 90 days pay in lieu of notice. At that time canned products for Crosse & Blackwell and supermarket giants ASDA, Sainsbury and Tesco were being produced at Lowestoft. The closure did not apply to the recently completed sauce, pickle, food dressing and ready meal operations.

In January 1997, F. E. Barber Ltd. was mentioned in the national press as one of five companies targeted by plotters who threatened to contaminate food produced by the company with micro-organisms that would cause severe pain and possible death to consumers. The scheme was to extort £250,000 from the five manufactures and to reinforce the seriousness of the threat, dye was injected into selected lines in various shops and phials were sent to the companies containing the harmful bacteria Yesinia Enterocolitica.

No longer part of the CWS, the modern waterside complex complete with the Barber Richmore name and logo, remained in production until late 1997 when that too was closed with the loss of 100 jobs. Many former employees and local folk will remember the location of this building as the site of the CWS sports ground and pavilion, on the north side of the No. 1 factory. The operating company, by that time Premier Foods Group subsidiary Chivers Hartley, stated that the Lowestoft operation was not viable and according to press releases issued at the time, the production was moved from Lowestoft to a factory at Bury St. Edmunds, which was considered a more accessible unit.

The closure had been expected by many following the announcement in February 1997 by the Managing Director of Chivers Hartley, Mr. Steve Orchard, that the company was reviewing the viability of their Lowestoft operation.

Immediately following the closure, a farewell party was held by former workmates at the Gluepot public house in Belvedere Road. Within a few years the Gluepot would be demolished to make way for a new road alignment, as the regeneration of the town progressed.

During October 1998, demolition commenced of the older No. 1 factory, warehouse and open storage area. Planning approval was granted in March 1999 by Waveney District Council for the regeneration of the former No. 1 factory site. This included demolition of some of the few remaining buildings, the refurbishment of others, and the establishment of a large motor dealership. Surprisingly, with predicted rising sea levels, flood defences do not appear to have been considered in the planning approval at this waterside location. One large building with CWS and Barber associations remains adjacent to the former No. 1 factory location. Of modern design, this building was the last food production unit to close and is currently used by Waveney Forklifts.

During April 1999 it was announced that the East of England Development Agency had purchased the larger No. 2 factory site for redevelopment as a job creating business park. It was envisaged that 450 new jobs would be created there when the park was fully developed. The scheme was part of a £3.6 million regeneration scheme and the local MP, Mr. Bob Blizzard, was reported as describing the demolition of the factory and the establishment of a business park as "the best news Lowestoft has had for years".

Following the demolition of most of the No. 2 factory buildings, the well known local landmark, the 160ft. factory chimney, was demolished between 25th - 29th March 2000. For many years a familiar sight in the town with its statuesque presence, the chimney had provided local people with a constant reminder of the once thriving food processing and canning factories that had employed thousands of people through generations of local families.

At the time of writing (late 2007), it is proposed that the land formerly accommodating the large three storey CWS factory building, storage area, railway siding and a group of CWS owned terraced houses will be used for the "Waveney Campus", a vast public sector complex for the use of Waveney District Council, Suffolk County Council and the government marine research body CEFAS. It is reported that the building will be designed to accommodate 1,000 employees and was quoted by the East of England Development Agency in January 2007 as costing at least £53 million. The occupants of the new complex would move from other buildings in the town and elsewhere. The remaining part of this large site has been used to accommodate the Riverside Business Centre, a small office block accommodating start up and small local companies and, adjacent to Waveney Drive, a children's nursery.

As already mentioned, the CWS subsidiary F. E. Barber Ltd. was purchased by Hobson plc for a sum in excess of £104 million and included in the deal were a number of CWS factories that had traditionally supplied hundreds of retail shops throughout the Co-operative movement with the Co-op own brand goods, and had produced own label brands for other leading food retailers. As part of the deal, Hobson plc, a leading manufacturer and supplier of own label foods and drinks, was awarded an exclusive food supply contract with the CWS until November 1999. This contract was later extended.

After the closure of the factories by Hobson plc, the CWS stated that F.E. Barber Ltd. was sold as a going concern to Hobson plc and had they known that Hobson would close the Lowestoft factories they would have kept them. The CWS had spent over £15 million on modernising the factories in the ten years prior to the closure by Hobson plc.

Hillsdown Holdings, the last owner of the nearby Lowestoft canning and food manufacturer Morton's, later acquired Hobson plc. Morton's closed in 1988 having been established in 1901 and produced a selection of food products some of which were similar to those produced at the Lowestoft CWS factories, although the range was not as extensive or varied as that illustrated elsewhere in this book.

A DETAILED DESCRIPTION OF THE CO-OPERATIVE WHOLESALE SOCIETY FACTORIES AT LOWESTOFT

The following pages are a direct copy, reproduced in this book by kind permission of Co-operative Group (CWS) Ltd. in Manchester, of an official guide to the Lowestoft CWS factories. Reference is made in the guide to the River Waveney being adjacent to the factories, this of course is **Lake Lothing**. Some of the pages are marked due to old age and poor storage, but the information and images contained in this rare publication are irreplaceable and give a wonderful insight into the workings of one of the many sadly missed industrial giants of Lowestoft.

The HOME of WAVENEY PRODUCTS

— · —

A Description of the
Co·operative Wholesale Society Limited's
Canning & Preserved Food Factories,
Waveney Drive,
Lowestoft.

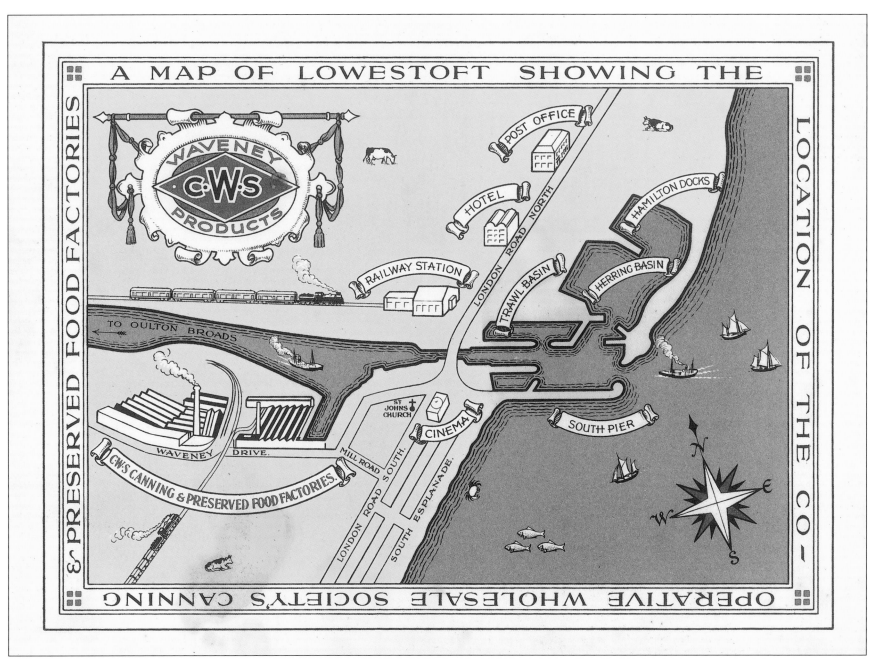

PRESERVED FOOD FACTORIES

LOCATION OF THE CO-

OPERATIVE WHOLESALE SOCIETY'S CANNING &

WAVENEY CWS PRODUCTS

POST OFFICE

HOTEL

HAMILTON DOCKS

RAILWAY STATION

LONDON ROAD NORTH

TRAWL BASIN

HERRING BASIN

TO OULTON BROADS

ST JOHNS CHURCH

CINEMA

SOUTH PIER

WAVENEY DRIVE.

CWS CANNING & PRESERVED FOOD FACTORIES.

MILL ROAD

LONDON ROAD SOUTH.

SOUTH ESPLANADE.

The Home of Waveney Products

FOREWORD

Once upon a time, in quite an ordinary street in the fishing-port of Great Yarmouth, there stood a small building, which proudly sported the sign: "Co-operative Wholesale Society Limited, Canning and Preserved Food Factory." An unpretentious structure—yet here was born and nursed a great idea.

The idea was to be a boon to the harassed housewife, who, when unexpected guests arrived, could fling open the doors of her heart and home to them, confident that on her shelves reposed enough eatables to feed them. In short, the idea was that of canning food, so that throughout the seasons one might partake of Mother Nature's bounties.

It was on those premises that the silver herring were first packed in the tins which bear for a trade-mark the smiling, bonnie face of Jennie, the Scotch fisher lassie, that is now known all over the British Isles.

And so the idea grew and grew until the tiny precincts of its birthplace limited its progress, and so in September, 1929, there was opened the spacious factory which we all know as the Canning and Preserved Food Factory, Waveney Drive, Lowestoft.

GREAT YARMOUTH CANNING FACTORY.
1918 TO 1929.

GUIDES.   FISH AND MEAT PASTES   LOADING
           LABELLING ROOM.   WAY.

We propose now to take you on a tour of inspection through the Factory. First of all, we must introduce you to one of our guides, who looks charming and capable in her pretty overall. As we follow her, we cross the covered loading way giving access to the quayside, which is some 365 yards long.

From here we are conducted to the Fish and Meat Paste Room. But who can resist a peep, as we go by, into that most intriguing of places—the Laboratory?

A shining array of utensils meets our wondering gaze, and a delicious aroma assails our nostrils. Still, believing there is better yet to come, we hurry on to watch how the machine apportions the paste to the jar, after which it is inspected by a girl to see there are no tiny air pockets, as these would ruin the product.

Twenty different varieties of Fish and Meat Pastes are prepared here and packed under the well-known brands— Wheatsheaf, Large and Small Unity, and Unity Tumblers. Millions of jars are produced annually.

Now when we mention that we are next going to visit the Kitchen, we cannot blame you if instantly you conjure up visions of important-looking chefs bustling to and fro, white enamelled electric stoves, and jars labelled "Flour," "Currants," &c.

And if that be so, you are going to have a surprise. Our Kitchen is a long room, a section of which is occupied by a number of steam-jacketed pans, which are used for the boiling of Soups and Tongues; also large tanks for the boiling of Brisket of Beef, and the materials used for the table delicacies such as Pressed Beef, Lunch Tongues, Picnic Tongues, Ox Tongues, and Chicken Breasts.

THE KITCHEN.

Mounting guard over these pans and tanks are the sensitive instruments known as Cambridge Recorders. Every varying temperature and time are recorded automatically upon a chart. Thus one is able to tell at a glance at what stage of cooking are the various commodities.

Also in the Kitchen we stand and watch the processing of the Gammons, which are placed in aluminium presses, where they are partly cooked, and then transferred to various sizes of cans before being hermetically sealed.

TINSMITH'S SHOP.   RETORT ROOM.

If we are of a mechanical turn of mind, our Tinsmith's Workshop will be a veritable paradise to us.

Here we notice how the lids are spun, by means of the irregular seaming machine, on to the gammon tins. This is an interesting process, for if we are fortunate enough to see a tin opened, it will be seen that the edges of the lid and the can are interlocked.

The gammon tins are next deposited into a huge vacuum machine, which draws out all the air. The tins pass slowly under a giant soldering iron, and this finally seals and renders them air-tight.

Many operations of a similar nature are also performed in connection with the packing of other commodities.

As we leave the Tinsmith's Shop to the next Department, our ears are assailed with the clanging of huge, iron doors, and we wonder what is now in store for us.

Here are rows of Retorts for the cooking and sterilisation of the commodities. Trays of glasses of Fish and Meat Pastes, still other trays of Canned Peas or Beans, Canned Gammons, Tongues, and, when in season, Herrings in Tomato. All these things pass into the enormous ovens, where they are cooked under steam pressure and thoroughly sterilised. Again we see the Cambridge Recorders, with their mechanical pen, registering the temperature to which the food-stuffs are subjected throughout the process.

We should see the earlier history of the peas before we go to the Canning Department. On a warm summer's day, it is a pleasant sight to watch the lorries, with their loads of swinging, laden pods, draw up near the vining machine, and see the precious produce tipped into the open, inviting mouth. Once swallowed, the peas are whirled around the huge interior, and from one side comes pouring all the waste—empty shells, &c.—and from the other the perfectly shelled peas.

At this stage the peas are transferred to a huge washing and grading machine. The grading is accomplished by three cylindrical drums, which are perforated with holes to the size of peas required. On they go to the cooking process; the picking tables, where eager-eyed girls snatch out the undesirables; and the filling and seaming machines, which fill the cans with liquid and peas, or beans, set the lids on the cans, and seam them up at the rate of 130 per minute. Still they are not ready to face the world, but go to the retort house, where all food-stuffs in glass and tin are further cooked and sterilised. Our productivity is amazing, many millions of tins of peas and beans being prepared annually!

An outward cleansing for the shining little tins, then on to the labelling room, where they collect their attractive labels at the rate of 80 per minute. Finally, into the outer cases are packed the peas that will please the palate of an epicure.

GATHERING PEAS.   VINING MACHINE.   CANNING PEAS.

"JENNIE."

Jennie was a Scotch lassie. One of a band of cheery, hard-working people, who annually leave their homes and follow the shimmering shoals of herring round our island.

We picture her at Lowestoft, with her companions, gutting the fish in the rapid way of all Scotch lassies, flinging them with dexterity and accuracy into their own particular tub, never ceasing from her labours, and always with that happy little smile playing about her lips or else singing some gay song.

And, thanks to our enterprising camera-man, that smile is able to greet all and sundry who purchase a tin of "Jennie" Herrings.

In the Factory we pause at the troughs where the girls stand packing the tempting little fish, and note the process. The fish are weighed, so that every tin gets the right contents. They are then laid neatly inside by expert fingers. Tomato puree is added, and a machine seams up the tin; and so we have the completed dainty.

The Press Room is our next objective; and here we see the heaps of gleaming tinplates which come from South Wales, and are manufactured from the best British metal.

With amazement we watch the tinplates being submitted to the lacquering process, followed by falling into the clutches of that sturdy iron monster, the gang-slitter, whose steely shears cut through the sheets of tin as though they are silver paper.

Now to the toggle press, which, with its gracefully gliding die, irresistibly impresses and cuts the style of tin required. And, hey presto! into the receptacle provided for the purpose, falls the tin on the first stage of its momentous career as container of a Waveney Production or "Jennie" Herrings.

Being a modern Factory, "No Waste" is our motto. We have, therefore, an ingenious machine, which is filled with old, unwanted cans, strippings of metal, &c. Pressure is brought to bear upon it, more waste material and more pressure are added, and, when the victims of the press are liberated at last, they are in one solid mass, which is now for sale for further usefulness.

TOGGLE PRESS.

"OFF TO-DAY—THERE TO-MORROW."

The long, lofty room is a veritable hive of industry. Here is animation! There is realisation that the harvest of the sea and soil is garnered in, and the determination that, without delay, the Co-operative Societies must have their shelves stocked with Waveney Productions. We visitors feel that we have suddenly stumbled in upon a busy railway station, peopled with hefty Herculeses hauling trucks about, laden with huge packing-cases. We hear the sonorous clang of the hammer beating out its challenge to the porters, vanmen, &c., who help the productions on their way to the outside world.

There is, however, one peaceful corner in the room, and that is where we are privileged to watch the deft play of the girls' fingers as they fasten the labels around the jars of paste, their eyes carefully scrutinising each finished little jar before it is carefully and compactly tucked away in the commodious packing-case.

Distinctive labels are splashed on to the cases, and back once more we go to the clatter and clamour, as we follow the giants which are transporting the cases to the adjoining private railway siding. In they go—the cases destined to reach important city, large town, small town, village, and tiny hamlet. With a puff and a snort the solid, capable engine starts into movement, and, shading our eyes, we watch the stream of trucks—proudly labelled "C.W.S. LOWESTOFT PRODUCTIONS"—steaming out of our sight round a bend in the railroad.

A green expanse, some three acres in extent, bounded on one side by the sturdy walls of the Factory and on the other by the smoothly-flowing River Waveney, such is the Sports Ground as revealed to our eyes when we push open the stout gate. Containing, as it does, three beautiful tennis courts; a cricket, football, and hockey pitch; a bowling-green; and a capacious well-fitted pavilion, the ground proves a great attraction to the employees, who spend many of their leisure hours in happy and healthy exercise.

The youth of the Canning Factory is enticed to the tennis nets, and a chorus of merry, triumphant cries as a timely shot is scored, together with the sharp ping of ball upon racquet, greets our ears. Some, however, prefer the joys of "the willow," and their white-clad figures streak with athletic grace across the soft green grass. The veterans choose the slow soothing skill of bowling, and we watch a group amicably arguing over the distance between two of the "ends," while their cronies sit placidly smoking and listening on a nearby bench.

We walk through the pavilion, with its shady lounge and comfortable dressing-rooms, complete with shower sprays; and then we sit on the sunlit verandah gazing at the vivacious picture before us. The shabby little tramp steamers chug-chug-chug up the broad bosom of the Waveney, smaller boats float silently by, and then a boatload of pleasure-seekers wave their hands in friendly greeting to the happy throng on the Sports Ground.

And we onlookers muse on how sweet life can be.

SPORTS FIELD.   SPORTS PAVILION.

POWER HOUSE.

We enter the Boiler House, whose six huge Lancashire boilers constitute the energy of the Factory and generate the steam and electricity for the manufacturing processes; and we decide that there is a certain allure about it all—the heaps of coal, the grimy figures of the stokers, and the towering bulk of the boilers. The stoker obligingly opens one of the doors, and, leaning back on his shovel, watches our expressions, with the avid attention of a showman, as we gaze into the inferno with its cascades of golden sparks dancing above the roaring, blazing fires. A hot breath darts out at us, and then the door is banged, shut again, and we are left to stare at the stalwart stoker who feeds this fiery steed. What a satisfaction it must be to hear the muffled roar that greets each shovelful of fuel, and to know that one is playing one's part by stirring to activity the machines in the processing departments !

We step through a doorway, and a transformation scene meets our gaze. A serene, silent, and dignified room is the Power House, with its cool, white walls and granolithic floor, and the smoothly-running motors. The electricity for machinery and lighting throughout the Factory is generated here. The switchboards look very awesome. The stalwart stoker loves his boilers, but the energetic engineer worships his various mystic machines, for standing before one of them, as before a shrine, is a vase of flowers.

A number of huge boilers filled with sizzling fat, where potatoes sliced to a shred dance and whirl in frantic fantastic glee!

Each pan is presided over by a cook in a becoming blue overall, who shakes and shuffles the golden fragments until they are crisp and crunchy.

We have already seen the peeling and washing-machines, and the cute little machine into which one puts a whole potato, that comes out cut into slices complete with a permanent wave—cut, crimped, and curled!

Now, the frying-pans draw us irresistibly, and we stand around like a pack of hungry schoolboys while the tempting morsels are poured from the pans.

COOKING POTATO CRISPS.

After draining, the crisps, with a tiny packet of salt, are piled into the grease-proof bags decorated with a photograph of the Norfolk Broads.

No wonder crisps, born in such a beautiful setting, reign triumphant in the realm of snack dainties.

Entering the main building of No. 2 Factory, we proceed to the top storey to see for ourselves the production of Waveney Soups, which include Kidney, Mock Turtle, Onion, Ox Tail, and Tomato, with many more varieties.

WAVENEY CHEESE (GRINDING).

The first sensation of which we are aware is a sharpening of the appetite, caused by the fragrance of the Soups being mixed and dried in the steam-jacketed pans.

From the pans, the ingredients are conveyed to the grinding machines, then to the filling and weighing apparatus, where they are placed in the small packets and the familiar cardboard containers.

Familiar, indeed, are all these Waveney Specialities to the mother, who knows how to raise a shout of appreciation from her family by producing, on a cold winter's day, a plate of steaming Waveney Soup.

At the farther end of the room are the machines busily preparing and packing the Waveney Cheese.

We peer into the cauldrons where the creamy, golden mixture is bubbling and boiling, and our imaginations travel back to the source of origin. We visualise fat, sleek cows blinking in the warm sunshine and browsing with placid content in the cool, green meadows.

After this short flight of fancy, we watch, with the interest of the consumer, each developing process in turn, until we reach the last and most amazing machine of all. This machine cuts and compresses the tinfoil into shape, fills each container with cheese, covers with tinfoil, fixes the attractive label into

CANNED VARIETIES

TABLE DELICACIES IN GLASSES

PACKET VARIETIES

"WAVENEY" COOKED MEATS

TOP ROW (Left to Right)—Chicken and Ham Galantine.   Pressed Pork.   Chicken, Ham, and Egg Galantine.
SECOND ROW (Left to Right)—Veal and Ham Galantine.   Jellied Beef and Tongue.   Jellied Veal and Ham.   Veal and Ham a la mode. . Beef Loaf.
THIRD ROW (Left to Right)—Pork Brawn.   Beef a la mode.   Pork Brawn.   Glazed Ox Tongue   Veal Brawn.
FOURTH ROW (Left to Right)—Stuffed Veal.   Silverside Beef.   Cooked Gammon.   Glazed Brisket Beef.   Cooked Gammon.   Roast Pork.   Veal Loaf.
BOTTOM (Left)—Jellied Ham and Tongue.   BOTTOM (Right)—Jellied Veal, Ham, and Egg.
FRONT—Range of varieties in Pies and Sausages, also York Ham.

position, and finally turns out the finished portion, to be packed, with five more companions, into the round boxes of which 6,000,000 have been prepared this year.

With a glow of gratification we realise that, through the medium of machinery in alliance with science, this wonderful production, Waveney Cheese, is produced to enrich our table.

With a feeling of justifiable curiosity, we approach the department devoted to the manufacture of Waveney Sausage and Cooked Meats, all of which are gaining rapidly in favour throughout the country.

The Sausage, like the Sphinx, has always been surrounded with mystery; but, at last, the veil is to be drawn aside, so with eager footsteps we press forward.

But any illusions on the matter are soon dispelled, when we see the array of beautiful fresh meats on their way to the mincing-machine to be converted into sausages.

It is fascinating to watch the minced meat disappearing in the sausage machine, and the way in which it is forced into the close-fitting skin ready to receive it. And thus the Sausage is created!

The Cooked Meats have a special appeal of their own, as they present an inviting picture when pressed and jellied. They include such delicacies as Galantines, Veal à la Mode, Beef à la Mode, and Pressed Pork, &c.

PACKING AND LABELLING WAVENEY CHEESE.

MAKING AND BAKING WAVENEY PIES.

Our guide now leads us to the Bakery, with its prim air of spotless cleanliness.

We look attentively around at the bins of snowy flour, the shining mixing-machine with its tireless arms that knead the dough to the required condition, the machine that shapes the neat little luncheon rolls, the white-garbed girls working happily in unison, and the loaded trays of pies waiting to fill the shelves of the enormous electric oven.

All shapes, sizes, and kinds of pies can be seen—Pork, Veal and Ham, Veal Ham and Egg, and Beef.

What a blessing these pies have proved themselves to be. The hiker on the bleak moorland path; picnic parties dining al fresco by a tinkling, rippling stream; the motorist and the British workman—all are happy and secure in the knowledge that within their rucksacks, hampers, and parcels reposes the mainstay of a meal—a Waveney Pie.

When we idly finger the round boxes that contain the triangular portions of cheese, we little think of the process the box itself has undergone before it becomes such a gaily-labelled, useful article.

Therefore, when our guide conducts us to the Cheese Box-Making Department, it is with some surprise we note the rows of formidable-looking machinery and stacks and stacks of reels of thin cardboard, that so forcibly remind us of a huge publishing house in Fleet Street.

We watch how the reels are mounted on an ingenious contraption, and, after receiving a preparation called " doping," are automatically conveyed into the blanking-machine. This machine stamps out the blanks which are to form the boxes and lids, giving them a crimped edge to allow for the shaping in the process.

CHEESE BOX-MAKING.

We cross to the shaping-machine, and note how the blanks are contrived into the desired pattern, and how the small waste is flipped out into a receptacle ready to receive it.

Farther along the room are the machines which make the corrugated cushions that are set into the boxes, and the other similar gadgets which assist in completing the processes.

Millions of these boxes are turned out annually.

Thus we see that here is a factory which is self-contained, so far as it is able to display proudly its own productions in a box or a tin that has been shaped on its own premises.

SECTION OF DISPLAY-ROOM.

A large room bids us welcome. It looks rather like the store-room of the benevolent Father Christmas, packed with parcels from floor to ceiling—each parcel contains something to gratify the heart of any person, who has so painstakingly kept and counted his or her coupons given away with Waveney Productions.

Silken underwear and gossamer stockings, the more prosaic male wear like shirts and socks, overalls, handbags, wallets, and watches—all are here awaiting the magic coupons which send them to the tens of thousands of gratified co-operators all over the country.

With the arrival of the post, the staff is galvanised into activity. What a post! Three times a day the postman bends his willing back under a load of letters and coupons.

The coupons are counted and sorted, the modern Santa Claus selects and despatches each particular gift, and the co-operative homes bear material testimony to the popularity of Waveney Cheese, Wheatsheaf and Unity Fish and Meat Pastes.

We now pause in admiration on the threshold of a beautiful and charming room—the Display and Sale Room. Luxurious blue settees provide a vivid contrast to the cream walls. Polished floors, the soft green of palms, and artistic lighting, all delight the eye and throw into relief the modern display cases.

Here we see how effective the finished products look. The tempting gleam of pale Chicken Breasts through the aspic jelly, the soft pink of Pressed Tongues, the voluptuous body of the Luncheon Sausage, the shining splendour of the huge Gammon tins, the colourful labels upon the cans containing Peas, Beans, and Soups, all contribute their part to make a comprehensive picture of Waveney Productions.

SECTION OF DISPLAY-ROOM.

In this room thousands of buyers have shown their appreciation by placing large orders, which continue to build up the wonderful trade being done in this Home of Waveney Specialities.

ENTRANCE TO No. 2 FACTORY.

We have witnessed the hygienic manner in which the commodities are prepared and packed—from the scrupulous washing of all glassware and the perfecting polish of the tins, to the critical examination of the finished goods. We cannot, however, leave the Factory without judging for ourselves the facilities for the comfort and the health of the employees.

Let us enter No. 2 Factory through the entrance hall, which is beautifully tiled in black and white. Hanging plants and palms give a cool, restful atmosphere. A glass roof covers the hall, through which we catch a glimpse of blue sky. An artistic pine staircase leads to the Display and Sale Room. Several spacious and lofty offices are situated on the ground floor, and we observe the numerous windows through which the golden sunshine comes streaming; the modern office furniture, portable and light; the desk lamps, which throw out a white radiance when days are dark and dreary; the smoothly-running typewriters, over which the typists' fingers dance so merrily, and all the other labour-saving

devices of an up-to-date office; and the telephone room, which is one constant tinkle of bells as the various Societies 'phone their orders.

We advance into one of the rooms leading off the Hall. It is a Rest Room, which is tastefully furnished with long, lounge chairs and settees. If one is harassed with a head-ache, there are long blue-and-gold curtains which can be drawn to give a welcome shade. The Ambulance Room is adjacent, containing its big white box painted with a red cross. Rows of bottles holding smelling salts, eau-de-cologne, sal volatile, &c., stand upon the shelves. An efficient-looking nurse, in her immaculate uniform, is monarch of all she surveys. We inspect the Dressing-rooms, with their white, washable walls, gleaming chromium fittings, and rows and rows of hooks; the white cabinet fitted with bevelled mirror, and roomy cupboards and drawers for little accessories; and the pier-glass, which obligingly adjusts itself to any angle.

Surely, we meditate, everyone must be happy working in surroundings so ideal as these.

REST ROOM.   STAFF DINING-ROOM.

EMPLOYEES' ANNUAL SPORTS.

On a Saturday afternoon, when the summer sun is high in the sky, crowds of employees and their friends assemble on the magnificent Sports Ground to witness the year's marathon.

Achilles and Adonis could not have presented more manly beauty and fitness than these sons of our Eastern outpost, whilst the shades of Venus and Atalanta might look with envy on the display of femininity competing one with another in real sporting spirit in the events of the day.

Humour and excitement attend the throng as they view the many events. For hours in quick succession the starter's gun announces some fresh contest, and the competitors strain nerve and sinew in their efforts to win the coveted trophies. The Mary Cottrell Trophy is the aspiration of the day, for this distinguishes the best all-round feminine achievement, whilst in like manner is the Lesa Trophy for the men.

There are races of all descriptions: some short and swift, others more leisurely but none the less strenuous; departmental relay races, obstacle races, no matter what the contests, all enter into them with vigour and good humour, characteristic of real sportsmanship.

The response from the audience determines the nature of each event. The shouts of laughter occasioned by the humorous difficulties presented in the obstacle race, whilst " tipping the bucket " is at once a thrilling and side-splitting performance.

The Tennis and Bowling Trophies are being won and lost as these tournaments proceed in more systematic and, perhaps, dignified measures, but all in their way entering into the play with zest and earnestness.

Tea and an evening Social brings a happy day to its close, and we feel that whether at work or play, Co-operative employees give of their best.

EMPLOYEES' ANNUAL SPORTS.

Having thus described the C.W.S. Canning and Preserved Food Factories, let us now for a moment consider the surroundings of this home of Waveney Productions.

Within two or three minutes walking distance one reaches Lowestoft Promenade, with its wonderful sea front and South Pier.

From the Pier, a picturesque view may be gathered of the Yacht Basin dotted with steamers resting after battling with the fierce North seas; little tugs that chug methodically into harbour, and wait patiently until the long finger of the bridge is slowly lifted to allow them to pass up the Waveney. In the herring season the fishing smacks, with their brown flapping sails, dip their way to the dockside,

SOUTH BEACH, LOWESTOFT.   OULTON BROAD.   SOUTH PIER, LOWESTOFT.

where the shoals of glittering fish are sold by the auctioneers.

There are many attractions at Lowestoft for the thousands of visitors who pour into this easterly seaside resort. The splendid facilities for sea-bathing and the firm stretches of golden sand tempt one to luxuriate in the sunshine, of which Lowestoft holds one of the highest records in the British Isles.

Along the Promenade are shady gardens, tennis courts, and putting greens. At the further end of the town, along the main thoroughfare, are the beautiful gardens known as "Sparrows' Nest," in whose Pavilion many of the leading artistes of the day are engaged during the season.

LISTENING TO THE ORCHESTRA, SPARROWS' NEST, LOWESTOFT.   ESPLANADE AND SOUTH PIER, LOWESTOFT.   THE YACHT BASIN, LOWESTOFT.

SPARROWS' NEST
THEATRE,
LOWESTOFT.

VICTORIA BATHING
STATION,
LOWESTOFT.

SOUTH PIER ILLUMINATIONS.

In yet another direction is the glorious expanse of water—Oulton Broad—from where the various motor-boats, dinghies, &c., may ply at their ease through 200 miles of green waterways.

In the midst of this superb setting, the most easterly point of England, where the first rays of the rising sun greet the shores of these, our isles, are the C.W.S. CANNING AND PRESERVED FOOD FACTORIES, WAVENEY DRIVE, LOWESTOFT.

C.W.S. PRINTING WORKS, LONGSIGHT, MANCHESTER.

LIST OF LOWESTOFT PRODUCTIONS

SAUSAGES, PIES, AND COOKED HAMS

COOKED MEATS
BRAWNS, JELLIED GOODS, and GALANTINES in variety

CANNED MEATS
(for slicing)
ROLLED OX TONGUE
PICNIC OX TONGUE
BRISKET BEEF
COOKED GAMMONS
GALANTINE ROLL

WHOLE CHICKENS
(in cans)

CHICKEN BREASTS
(in Aspic Jelly)

TONGUES (in glass moulds)
ROLLED OX
SLICED OX
PICNIC OX (Calves)
"SANDRINGHAM" (Calves)
LUNCH (Lambs)

MEATS (in glass moulds)
SPICED BEEF AND TONGUE
BEEF AND TONGUE
(without spice)
JELLIED BRAWN
BOAR'S HEAD
GALANTINE

"JENNIE" BRAND
HERRINGS IN TOMATO
HERRINGS IN OIL
HERRINGS FRESH
HERRING ROES

"WAVENEY" CRUST-LESS CHEESES
CHEDDAR CHEESE
CHESHIRE CHEESE
SANDWICH CHEESE
CHEESE AND CELERY
WELSH RAREBIT

"WILLOWVALE" CHEESE AND TOMATO

"UNITY" CHEDDAR CHEESE

"UNITY" AND "WHEAT-SHEAF" FISH AND MEAT PASTES
in 24 varieties

CANNED VEGETABLES
"WAVENEY" FRESH PICKED PEAS (National Mark)
"UNITY" BRAND GREEN PEAS (Reprocessed)
"WAVENEY" BEANS AND TOMATO
"WAVENEY" BUTTER BEANS
"WAVENEY" STRINGLESS BEANS

"WAVENEY" SOUPS
(Liquid, in cans)

"WAVENEY" SOUPS
(Powder, in packets)

"GRAVIN" GRAVY POWDER (in packets)

POTATO CRISPS

C·W·S CANNING &
PRESERVED FOOD FACTORIES,
LOWESTOFT.

Factory and Railway Scenes

Top Left - The No. 1 factory chimney is prominent in the centre of this unusual view from the No. 2 factory in the 1930s. This chimney was removed in the 1950s. *(Courtesy Don Powell)*

Top Right - This lady is checking beans or peas and removing any found unsuitable for canning, a job also undertaken on conveyor belts with teams of ladies doing the inspecting. Perhaps not the most exciting job, but vital in maintaining the high quality of CWS products. *(Courtesy Don Powell)*

Bottom Left - Both factories were decorated for the 1935 Jubilee and this view of the No. 2 factory shows the extent to which the CWS went, including flags across the road to the General Managers house. One fine motor car of the period and a well dressed group of folk complete this midday scene. *(Courtesy Peter Killby)*

Another interesting view of the factories in 1935 whilst decorated for the Silver Jubilee of King George V and showing a traffic free Waveney Drive. *(Courtesy Peter Killby)*

The factories again in 1935 but showing an abundance of smoke from the No. 1 factory chimney being blown across Waveney Drive. *(Courtesy Don Powell)*

The large display lounge in the No. 2 factory included this demonstration shop with a fine display of Lowestoft products. The assistant is holding a canned chicken. *(Courtesy Don Powell)*

An early 1950s scene in the area known as the Pea Fields with pea viners at work. Vining at this location ended in the early 1960s after which it was transferred to the farms. *(Courtesy Don Powell)*

Most people who worked at the factories in the 1930s, during World War Two and in the 1940s fondly remember the happy days there. These scenes were recorded during that period.

Top Left - A group of girls from the No. 1 factory with one holding an empty can. These cans were used to deliver tomato puree to the factories; many more cans are behind the girls. From left to right, the first names of those in the photograph are:- unknown, Cathie, Agnes, Audrey (upper), Flossie (lower), Alice and Doris.

Top Right - A larger group of girls from the No. 1 factory in front of the Sports Pavilion in the summer of 1938. *(Top left and right photographs courtesy Florence "Flossie" Baldry)*

Bottom Left - The CWS estate was vast and often visiting parties could be as many as 300 people. A large number of tour guides was required to cope with this number of visitors and this 1947 photograph shows the usual 14 guides together with a few extras. On the back row from left to right are: - unknown, Joyce Catchpole, Mabel Hutchinson, Edna ?, Gwenneth Lewis, unknown, Kate ?, Thelma ?, Beatrice Woods, Dot Mingay, Audrey ?, unknown, unknown. On the front row are:- Joan Reynolds, Mollie Thacker, Trixie Bartram, unknown, unknown. *(Courtesy Gwenneth Maclean)*

Conducted tours of the factories were always popular and in many cases the groups of people wishing to see the factories travelled long. distances by road or rail. A group of factory tour guides are seen in the 1940s with a coach that had brought a party of visitors to Lowestoft for a visit. From left to right are, unknown, Audrey Curtis, Joyce Catchpole, Mabel Hutchinson, Molly Thacker, Dot Mingay, Kate ?, and Beatrice Wood (Head Guide). *(Courtesy Mabel Haylock)*

The CWS Hall in Riverside Road was an important community asset used for many functions, including this children's party in the 1950s. *(Courtesy Don Powell)*

For many years, after being cut the pea crop was brought straight from the fields to the factories and this scene shows peas being hand fed into the battery of factory located viners. These separated the peas from the pods and in later years were located at the farms.
(The Malcolm White Collection)

An early 1950s view of a section of one of the factory warehouses with Waveney products ready to leave for co-operative societies throughout the country either direct or via a CWS depot or warehouse. The well known CWS "Waveney" brand view of a river complete with two wherries can just be seen on the boxes.
(The Malcolm White Collection)

A scene in the No. 1 factory during the early 1950s showing one of the newly installed fast operating machines that filled and sealed the cans. In this case the cans are being filled with either beans or peas, a few of which can be seen in the bottom left of the picture.
(The Malcolm White Collection)

Brian Peak and Eric Ellis working on a seamer, a machine used to seal the lid of a can to the can body, in the No. 2 factory.
(Courtesy Don Powell)

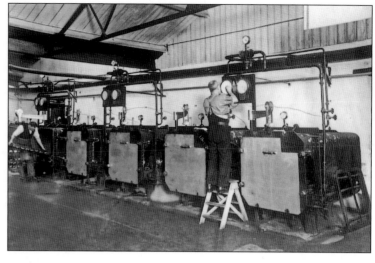

Top Left - Broad Bean podders seen at Lowestoft in 1962. These were only used for a limited period each year, but remained in situ.

Top Right - A few of the many retorts in the No. 1 factory at Lowestoft in the 1950s. These were used to heat process batches of cans at high temperature using steam. A tray of cans can be seen being either put in or being removed from the retort on the left.

Bottom Left - Ladies at work in the No. 1 factory preparing and filling cans with beans or peas on a production line in the 1950s.

(All photographs Courtesy Don Powell)

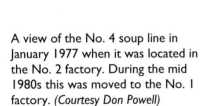

At one time three brands of cheese products, "Willowvale", "Unity", and "Waveney" were made at Lowestoft. In the No. 2 factory, we find Violet Chipperfield packing portions of "Willowvale" cheese spread into boxes ready for dispatch to stores across the country. *(Courtesy Geoffrey Moore)*

A view of the No. 4 soup line in January 1977 when it was located in the No. 2 factory. During the mid 1980s this was moved to the No. 1 factory. *(Courtesy Don Powell)*

The Costing Office staff at Lowestoft in the early 1960s. From left to right in the front row are Joan Reynolds, unknown, and June Sutherland.
In the back row are Lesley ?, Ted Duckworth, Lynn Banham, unknown, Douglas Poole and Andrew Baldwin.
(Courtesy Margaret Duckworth)

The CWS at Lowestoft had a large Transport Department and some of those involved in that department are seen here in the 1970s. From left to right are unknown, unknown, Claude ?, Trevor Burns, Tom Cummings, unknown, Factory Manager Peter Lomen, unknown, unknown, Michael Last, Ron Knights, Arthur Balls, Bill Rose, Ted Duckworth, unknown, Peter Crawford, unknown, unknown, Reg Miller, Jill ?, unknown, unknown.
(Courtesy Margaret Duckworth)

The Kirkley railway branch line served many large firms based in south Lowestoft as well as the Kirkley Goods Depot at the bottom of Lovewell Road. For many years the CWS was a major user of the line with vast quantities of goods arriving and finished products leaving by the railway.

Top Left - At one time an every day sight in Kirkley as a train leaves Riverside Road and crosses Waveney Drive to return to Lowestoft. As well as serving other industrial complexes such as Brooke Marine, the train will no doubt have contained trucks loaded with CWS products for distribution across the country. On the left is the No. 2 factory and just visible a well known feature of Waveney Drive, the pumping station. The locomotive is Great Eastern Railway designed Class J17 0-6-0 No. 65558.

Top Right - A location totally changed with the opening of the South Lowestoft relief road. It is now impossible to trace this railway junction since the road cuts across the trackbeds, and the pleasant open area and wetlands that once existed in south Lowestoft. On the left is a Class J17 0-6-0 locomotive with a train from the lakeside/CWS line and on the right is a another Great Eastern Railway designed locomotive, Class J15 0-6-0 No. 65389 involved in shunting trucks at the Kirkley Goods Depot. This handled coal, general merchandise and when in season, large quantities of sugar beet grown at the many farms that once existed around Lowestoft. **Bottom Left** - Another view of this busy branch line as a train leaves Kirkley and heads for Oulton Broad South station and then on to Lowestoft. The trackbed at this point, between Notley Road and Kimberley Road, is now a path and cycle track.

All four locomotives seen on this page were based at Lowestoft for many years and after the withdrawal of steam traction, diesel locomotives took over the hauling of trains along the branch. Oil for the boilers in the No. 2 factory was one of the last items carried over the branch for the CWS. (All photographs courtesy Chris Moss/The Dr. Ian Allen Collection)

Showtime
Presented by the Employees

CWS Hall, Riverside Road,
Lowestoft

The factories had a vibrant drama and entertainment group who put on a varied programme of high quality performances that included variety shows, musicals, reviews and pantomimes in the excellent hall adjacent to the No. 2 factory.

The facilities of the hall, including the catering, were made available for these well supported events. In addition, entertainment was provided for children's parties and social events.

Above are scenes from a performance of Snow White and the Seven Dwarfs and on the **left** we see the cast of a Minstrel Show complete with their blackened faces.

(All photographs The Cathryn White/Joe Sharman Collection)

Showtime
Presented by the Employees

CWS Hall, Riverside Road,
Lowestoft

Further examples of the popular entertainment provided by members of the Lowestoft factories workforce in the CWS Hall. The photographs **above** show the cast of a Minstrel Show and on the **right** are some of the cast of a review in a scene that has an eastern theme. The gentleman on the right is Joe Sharman, well known at the factories for his involvement in these shows.

The substantial CWS Hall was demolished as part of the scheme to establish a business park on the site of the No. 2 factory.
(*All photographs The Cathryn White/Joe Sharman Collection*)

Gwenneth Maclean (nee Lewis)
No. 1 Factory 1943-49
No. 2 Factory 1935-40

I started working for the Co-operative Wholesale Society (CWS) at their Lowestoft No. 2 factory when I was 16 years old and was paid 5/- (25p) per week. Initially I worked in the cheese box making department on the ground floor of the building where the foreman was Mr. George Ellis. The other girls in that department were Ruby Banham, Katharine "Trixie" Bartram, Irene Coleby, Dorothy Farman, Doris Harness, Iris Harper, Lilias Highway, Myra Highway, Evelyn Lee, Marjorie Proudfoot, Evelyn Yallop and also Dorothy and Pamela whose surname I do not know. Five or six of us from that department went cycling together at weekends.

The factory bakery was also situated on the ground floor with Mr. George Massey as foreman. By the time I was 18years old, my pay had been increased to £1 per week. After 4½ years in the cheese box making department, I was transferred for six months to the dry soup department on the top floor of the factory where Mr. Frank Jones was our foreman. My job was to put the powder mix into the cartons ready for sending out to the shops. The cooked cheese room was also on the top floor where Mr. Alfred Church was the foreman. On the first floor could be found the sausage room where the foreman was Mr. Eddie Jessop. Also on this floor with Mr. Johnnie Orton as foreman, was the large cooked meats department. The factory manager at this time was Mr. Crawley.

In 1940, some of us left the CWS at Lowestoft and went to work in a large factory at Solihull where we assembled aircraft engines for the Royal Air Force. Others left the factory around the same time and went to work at Letchworth. Later in the war, the Lowestoft CWS factories were considered essential to the war effort and no further employees left there for other work. After three years at Solihull I heard that nobody was leaving the Lowestoft factories because of their importance and sent a letter to CWS factory director Mr. Wilkinson requesting a move back to my home town.
This was agreed and I was released from working at Solihull and

returned home to Lowestoft and the CWS in 1943 when I was 24. Initially I worked in the No. 2 factory with a group of Italian prisoners of war on tray packing dried vegetables for the troops before moving across the road to the No. 1 factory. During the war years we frequently had to stop work and get to the air raid shelter in No. 2 factory as quickly as possible as enemy fighters and bombers swooped down and machined gunned and bombed the town.

The No. 2 factory had anti-aircraft guns on the roof as well as the air raid sirens which were used to warn folk of an attack. The No. 1 factory sustained substantial damage in the retort room during one of these attacks and amongst the workforce there were a number of fatalities and several people received injuries. However we carried on as best as we could, determined not to be beaten by the enemy. We worked two shifts, 0600hrs - 1400hrs and 1400hrs - 2200hrs, on alternate weeks during the war years, and for a few weeks following the end of the war. For the next six years I worked on the pea and bean lines where my pay was between £4 and £6 per week and where Mr. Tom Woodrow was our foreman. At this time in the No. 1 factory there was also the meat paste room, the ox tongue and other meats department, with Forewomen Nellie Holmes in charge. The beetroot and other vegetables department with Rose Larter in charge were also in the No. 1 factory.

The autumn herring season was a very busy time at the CWS when thousands of tins of "Jennie" brand herrings in tomato sauce, herrings in oil, fresh herring and herring roes left the production lines. Whilst the CWS factories at Lowestoft were well known throughout the country and abroad for their many fine products, it was probably the "Jennie" brand herring products that we were best known for. We had a large loading shed for the trains and lorries to go into and load up.

During my time at the No. 1 factory I was asked if I would like to be a CWS factory guide. It was a special privilege and honour to be a guide, and also very enjoyable since you met a great many different people in the large number of parties that visited the two factories on conducted tours. There were 14 of us available to act as guides at Lowestoft and on one occasion I remember we had 300 managers from the north visit the factories. This was a great many people but we managed and I think they enjoyed their visit to what was then one of the largest canning and food processing factories in the world. When the visitors to the factory had lunch and often tea in the restaurant the guides waited on them. For each occasion we did this we were paid an extra £2. That was a lot of money in those days.

The food was provided free of charge to visitors and was of course produced by the CWS!

A lot of the materials we used at the CWS came direct into the factories by the railway and most of the products we made there were loaded on to trains in the goods shed and sent away. I lived in Victoria Road and remember seeing long trains travelling to and from the factories every day along the railway line opposite the front of our house.

I left the factory in 1949 when I got married.

Sitting second from left in the front row, Gwenneth is seen here with other tour guides and some members of a visiting party outside the No. 2 factory. The first names of the guides in the back row are from left to right:- Kate, Mabel, Edna, Joan, unknown. In the front row are: - Molly, Gwen, Beatrice (head guide), Joyce and Trixie. *(Courtesy Gwenneth Maclean)*

Gwenneth is sitting bottom centre of this group seen outside the works entrance of the No. 2 factory in Riverside Road. On the left is Dorothy Farman and on the right, Trixie Bartram. The name of the lady sitting above Gwenneth is unfortunately unknown.
(Courtesy Gwenneth Maclean)

"Waveney" products - By any test they're the best!

Ione Ellis (nee Rawston)
No. 1 Factory 1971-1983

Until 1959, I worked at the Eastern Coach Works in the stores office and after having a break from work, commenced working at the Lowestoft Cooperative Wholesale Society No. 1 Factory in 1971. I worked the afternoon half shift, which was either 1330hrs - 1630hrs or 1400hrs - 1800hrs, and the pay was around £5 per week.

My normal work was cutting the tops off carrots before they went into tanks of water prior to being put into the washer, where any remaining dirt was removed. The carrots were then ready for canning. We were given boxes containing hundreds of carrots and for each box we emptied, we received a small bonus of a few pence. Sometimes I was put on the pea line where many of us checked that all the peas were perfect before they were canned.

Another job I did was watching and checking the liquid going into cans after they had been filled with the different vegetables. We also canned runner beans in the No. 1 factory and mushrooms, which had to be steamed in order to sterilise them. Cans of mixed vegetables were another product prepared at the factory and one of the other jobs I was given, was to prepare the swedes before they were mixed with the other vegetables that made up the mixture.
On a production line it could be very noisy with the cans moving about and banging together, the washer going continuously and other machinery running. When working on a line, most of us had to stand all the time and carry out the same procedure many hundreds of times each week. We normally wore a blue overall, with a turban or net on our heads when working. I remember several others who worked at the factory including Gladys Reed who spent a lot of time on a machine where the can tops were put on, and many of those in charge of lines or who were supervisors, including Queenie Fuller, Dot Huron, Pamela Burlingham, and also Elsie, Iris and Mary. I am unable to remember the second names of these three.

Most of the machinery at the No. 1 factory was old and in need of replacing and we always knew that about 30 minutes or so into the shift, it was more than likely to break down. When this happened we would go and play in the cloakroom all afternoon. This we called our social club!

When there were no fresh vegetables available, we were given other work and had to go and work in other parts of the factory, or were sent over to the No. 2 factory. In the No. 2 factory we worked on pies, meat products, stews etc, and also soups.

A very unusual but regular job was working in the stores and wiping the crates of dusty tins and if the labels were too grubby, we had to tear them off to be replaced. We also had to polish the cans if they needed a good clean.

The CWS shop was in the No. 2 factory and this was open in the evening. We used to go there and get tins of vegetables, soup, stew, fruit and other food for only a few pence. Some of the tins had no label on and we were sometimes told that it contained something different to what we found when it was opened. Often you opened what was thought to be a tin of baked beans and found that it was fruit!

My friend and I agreed that the CWS soups were the best anywhere and these were made in Lowestoft. In addition to our own brand, the Lowestoft factories made many products such as canned peas for the major supermarkets including Tesco in the 1970s.

When I was very little, I lived in Durban Road and can remember the new factory being built, it really was massive.
When it finally opened, we were all invited to walk around the building and were given free samples of everything. It was a very large modern building and today there is nothing to remind us that it was ever there.

I left the CWS in 1983 when all part time workers had to leave, and got a job working at the Ross fish factory down by the Trawl Dock.

Florence "Flossie" Baldry (nee Meikle)
No. 1 Factory 1936-41

When I worked at the Lowestoft Co-operative Wholesale Society, I was in the paste room making potted meat and for most of the time at the factory I worked with the same group of girls on the line. The Forewoman was Alice Thompson and the factory manager at that time was Mr. Crawley. Although I cannot remember the actual amount, the pay at the factory was not a lot!

Only the girls in the mixing room started everyday on arrival, the rest of us always had our first job somewhere else in the factory until the potted meat was ready to be jarred. I used to clean Mr. Crawley's office first thing in the morning.

If my friend and I sneaked a half a day in the afternoon, we would usually go to the Odeon and sit in the cheapest seats which were at the front, because we had to make up our wages.
In 1938 I had appendicitis and as some of the jobs in other parts of the factory involved heavy lifting, I was assigned to the easy jobs in Mr. Crawley's office. Sometimes if he arrived before I had finished, we would have a cup of tea brought in for both of us.

In World War Two the factory was bombed, and we were sent home, I believe it was on a Saturday morning. Fortunately our room suffered only minor damage and I and the rest of us were sent for on the Monday to return to work. We were able to see the damage to the other parts of the factory and our room was back to work as usual in a very short time.

I left the factory in August 1941 when I got married and joined the NAAFI for several years working at Colchester and Southwold. My husband returned from Ceylon after 2½ years to fly Lancaster bombers and I was able to join him at his various RAF postings.

Sadly several of the girls have since passed away, but my special friend Ruby and I are still great friends although we do not see each other so often now.

Flossie is seen holding a bucket between two work mates at the Sports Pavilion in the late 1930s. They are suitably dressed for sterilising jars ready to be filled with potted meat or other products. Clothes and clogs such as those seen here were supplied where the work and floor in the factory was liable to be wet and slippery. *(Courtesy Florence Baldry)*

Don Powell
No. 1 and 2 Factories 1959-94

These are some of my memories during 34 happy years spent working at the Lowestoft CWS factories. I started there for the first time in March 1959 as a maintenance fitter. The chief engineer was Mr. R White with Laurie Bland as second in command followed by Mr. Harold Carver, a very clever engineer, but not cut out to be a leader. I began in what was known as the "Viner Gang", our charge hand was George Ellis, who was fine to work with but probably more interested in organising the annual concerts and carnival floats. We had a purpose built workshop at the east end of the long store which allowed two Mather and Platt viners to be backed in for their annual overhaul. Also working on the viners were Frank Jones, Harry Sirs and Terry Darby together with three fitters' mates, "Fussy" Smith, Harry Cook and "Franey" Martin. Fussy was the one whose job it was to make the tea/coffee. Tea breaks were 9am and 3pm, and the working day then was 7.30am to 12 noon and 1pm to 4.30pm, but as the Pea Season approached we would work till 7pm.

When a viner had been overhauled it would be towed out to Ellough by Jimmy Cross to be stored in one of the hangers which was also used to store thousands of sacks of dried beans and peas. The Pea Season would usually start sometime during the last week in June and the first week of July and last for about six weeks. I spent my first Pea Season looking after viners around Corton, Hopton, Lound and Flixton and on the Pound Farm Estate which, back in 1959, was farmed by Mr. Boardley. My mate that season was "Fussy" Smith, who was about 62 and totally reliable, someone who would always be there waiting to go out on the farms at 5am. He did not drive so I did the driving in a van the CWS hired for the season. Apart from repairing any breakdowns, we had to keep the viners topped up with diesel which we carried in a 40 gallon drum fixed in the back of the van. The viners were driven by a 3 cylinder Lister engine made in Peterborough.

The 1959 season was very hot and dry and I think the only rain we had was a Saturday morning in late July. In those days August Bank Holiday Monday was the first Monday in August. When I had to

work on the bank holiday it seemed very strange, but fresh peas only have about three days when they are at their best so we worked every day. When the last peas had been vined, the viners were brought back to the factory and stored at the back of No. 1 factory on what was known as the Pea Field, where they were stripped down and cleaned ready for overhauling once again.

Also on the Pea Field was what was known as the Carrot Shed, this was where all the carrots were washed before being taken down Riverside Road to the Carrot Room to be processed. While the carrot season was on, it was our job to make sure the washing plant in the carrot shed kept running. Working in this shed in the winter with a northerly wind was very cold as the shed had 2 sides and a roof but no ends.

Another recollection I have of my early days is of Frank Jones Jnr. first thing nearly every morning working on Laurie Bland's car in the viner shop, before "Chalkie" White made his morning rounds.

In 1963 Harry Sirs left to go to New Zealand and Terry Darby also left so we had Eric Ellis as replacement. We also lost "Fussy" Smith through retirement and he was replaced by George Chapman, known as "Chopper". By this time, the viners would work during the night out on the farms since we had six generators on trailers which were towed out to the farms to provide light for the viners. For several years the peas had been brought into the factory in aluminium trays, 28 pounds in a tray, but on a couple of farms they were trying out large tanks which held half a ton of peas. Several farms needed to get equipped to lift these tanks on to the lorry which then brought them into the factory to be washed and cleaned thoroughly before being pumped into tanks at the back of the cannery. Ernie Parker was the chargehand who would organise which tanks to use and what processing lines needed supplying with the peas and he had two very reliable operators to keep things running smoothly in Bobby Challis and George Turner. Walter Williamson was the number one factory superintendent with Jack Jillings and George Chamberlain as supervisors. In the 1960s we relied on retorts and two hydrostatic cookers to cook the peas. In charge of operating the two cookers was Wally Thrower who, in a cooker breakdown, was always a mine of information and most helpful.
During the 1950s, when these two cookers were new, Harold

Carver, then a fitter in can labelling, redesigned the infeed and discharge of the little cooker which made it work much better and the cooker manufacturers were pleased to modify their design to his.

Don in the workshop in September 1989.
(Copyright Don Powell)

In 1970, we had a new hydrostatic cooker installed known as the Stork Cooker which was made in Holland. This made the two existing cookers look very old and out of date and came complete with two new processing lines. With the processing lines running much faster, things had to change so the old Liquor Room which Charlie Ketless ran on the ground floor at the back of No. 1 Cannery was shifted up onto the Mezzanine floor with all new liquor tanks, pumps and glass liquor lines through to the liquid fillers. These glass

pipelines were OK for a time but became prone to leaks because of the number of joints in each line and since they were mainly all overhead were seen to be dangerous and eventually replaced with stainless steel piping.

With the liquor room shifting on to the floor where the can store was, new can lines were installed by Metal Box fitters from the long store to each line and also from the cookers to the can labellers. With the arrival of the Stork cooker a new pump room was needed and as the peas were now being vined by farmer owned viners, the viner workshop was used for the installation of a 9000 gallon tank and pumps plus the chlorination system. With the viner workshop gone our new home was the workshop which Percy Ellis and Herbert Burgess used while the pea cleaning plant was in use. This workshop was very close to my good blind friend, Stanley Freestone. He worked inside the long store bundling up sacks and also sorting out sacks which had holes; he would then repair them using Copydex and a piece of sack. Stanley was totally blind but to see him stack the sacks on to a pallet was really wonderful. As our new workshop was near to his workbench we rigged up a guide line for him to be able to come and have his break with us and get to the pea field toilet without having to rely on anybody. He thought this was wonderful. He was not the only one who would come for a break. Albert Besford, one of the painters, would also join us most afternoons along with Billy Watling, a fork lift driver. Bill Ledham, a Seamer workshop fitter, who was promoted to become second in command on the engineering side, would always find time to come for morning tea break with us. Bill was someone who never changed when he left to go on to the management side. He served under Laurie Bland and Cliff Trent but decided to leave the Co-op while the fitters and electricians were on their eight week strike in 1977. The strike ended when the engineers agreed to start back on shifts but the electricians remained on days.

The fitters in the cannery workshop during the 1960s and 70s were chargehand Dougie Burwood with Barry Hook, Brian Holland and Michael Walpole; Dave Sterry and Graham Betts came later. The fitters' mates were George Swan and Donny Hunting with Keith Powell and David Seago coming later.

The fitters in the can labelling workshop during the 1960s and 70s were Kenny Spinks, Dick Barton, who was a fighter pilot during the Second World War, and Percy Ellis, who shifted from the main workshop and their mates were Lou Burwood and Herbert Burgess.

The main workshop had George Leverick, Burt James, John Thurling, George Wilson, John Wilson, Ernie Holifield, Fred Robinson, and Brian Vine. There were others but I cannot recall their names. The mates were Derek Grice and Bob Dann and others I cannot put a name to.

In the garage we had Burt ?, Paul Barker, David Wright with David Prentice and David Hurr both apprentices and in the Electrician's shop there was Cyril Mayes, chargehand, who just before he retired at 65 could stand in front of the workbench and jump up on to it. There was also Arthur Crickmore and Jimmy Francis, who later became Personnel Manager and Bill Bailey, who could throw a cricket ball farther than most. In 1979, Terry Smith and others took on the CWS in a dispute over shifts and won the day. Tim Proctor, Kevin Blowers, Dick Lawn, Neil Andrews and Nigel ? came later. The mates who I can remember were Arthur Hunt and Alan Ife. The electrical supervisor in the later years was Alan Fathers who came from Birds Eye.

Frank Fiske was in charge on the building maintenance side in the 1960s and 70s, with Kenny Crowe as charge hand. The carpenters were Arthur Sullivan, Fred Parnell, and Ronnie Dalton, who was the CWS football team goalkeeper in the 1950s, "Little" Jimmy Whitehill, Alan Oxley, Geoff Ward and Tom Platten, who later was in charge of the building maintenance team that included the painters, Gordon Elsegood, Albert Besford, Billy Nicols and Reggie Ayres. The bricklayers were Charlie Atherton and Fred Brown. There was always one plumber on site, the longest serving one being Bernard Welby backed up by his mate Leo Bunn.

In the late 1970s with Bill Ledham leaving, the Chief Engineer Mr. Trent had Mr. George Brown as his deputy on Maintenance. In No. 2 factory were Frank Jones, supervisor, Brian Peak, Monty Blake, Peter Baker, Bob Jillings with Basil Woolley, David Seago and Stanley Upson as mates. I recall one afternoon while working in No. 2 factory helping Monty Blake set up the Christmas pudding line and while Monty went to find a missing part, I ate the only pudding which had been saved for setting up the machine.

The boiler house during my time was situated in No. 2 factory along Riverside Road. Billy Coleman was the fitter in charge and

when he retired Frank Jones took his place to be followed by Jimmy Keable from Great Yarmouth. When Jimmy retired Peter Mobbs became the last fitter to run the boiler house.

The factory went on to shifts in the late 1970s when there was a need for more fitters and, with the closure of Matthes Bakery in Gorleston, the CWS was able to provide jobs for several of the bakery's fitters.

The supervisors on the engineering side were John Jullings and Paul Russell in No. 1 factory with Frank Jones and Dave Gurney in No. 2 factory. They were supported by charge hands Colin Staff and Norman Rodwell, with several of the fitters previously mentioned plus Paul Rose, Tony Banthorpe, Jack Tuck, Dave Beamish, Peter Goreham, Graham Lay, Dave Peck, and Peter Holland. There were also four night fitters, Paul Barker, Terry Poll, Billy Ward and John Fox, who was later to become the Lowestoft Lifeboat Coxswain.

In the late 1980s and early 90s we saw the Ready Meals Department run for a short period followed by the Sauces and Pickles Factory. Both ran for a while following the sudden closure of the rest of the former CWS Factory on 14th October 1994.

A selection of canned vegetables produced at Lowestoft
in the early 1950s.
(The Malcolm White Collection.)

Factory Scenes

The CWS invested heavily in Lowestoft during the 1980s and early 1990s with the Ready Meal complex being one example of their investment programme. This officially opened in 1989 with part of the complex being housed in a new building which is seen here under construction. Part of the No. 1 factory pea cleaning plant can be seen in the bottom left.
(Copyright Don Powell)

Work underway in preparation for the new £multi-million Sauces and Pickles factory in 1989. This view is looking north and shows the area that one time was the CWS Tennis Courts and Sports Field. The stern trawler *Boltby Queen* and two beam trawlers belonging to Talisman Trawlers can be seen at North Quay. As with the CWS factories, the local fishing industry and the large fleet of fishing vessels is now only a memory.
(Copyright Don Powell)

Another view recorded in 1989 of groundwork underway in preparation for the construction of the Sauces and Pickles factory and looking towards the existing factories. The photograph was taken in the vicinity of where the Sports Pavilion once stood. *(Copyright Don Powell)*

Just prior to his retirement, painter Albert Besford is seen with a group of his workmates in the Paint Store on 9th February 1989. This store was situated in the Old Viner Shop on the Pea Field. *(Copyright Don Powell)*

Doboy packaging machinery and Slatband conveyors were installed in March 1989 for use in the shrink wrapping of products. This view shows the installation of this plant which had a relatively short life at Lowestoft, before being recovered for use elsewhere after the change of ownership and subsequent closure. Products were shrink wrapped prior to being palletised. Maintenance Fitter Peter Goreham pauses for a moment whilst working on the new plant. *(Copyright Don Powell)*

The summer of 1989 saw work in progress on the Sauces and Pickles factory with the steel framework of the building being assembled. On the other side of Lake Lothing and behind the jibs of the cranes can be seen the trawler LT30 *Ripley Queen*, the last vessel of that type to work from any east coast port. *(Copyright Don Powell)*

74

Top Left - An interesting view of the CWS Hall in Riverside Road through a gate in the No. 1 factory boundary wall. This gate was later bricked up. The hall was used extensively for a variety of purposes including dances, variety shows, boxing tournaments, parties and dining. After closure of the factories, the hall was used for jumble sales and the weekly diners club before being demolished. *(Copyright Don Powell)* **Top Right** - Part of the old liquor room in August 1989 showing a can opener and can crusher used to extract tomato puree from the cans, which were then crushed ready for re-cycling. *(Copyright Don Powell)* **Bottom Left** - Head Fieldsman Gordon Parker retired in September 1989 and is seen here in his office on the Pea Field in his last week at the CWS. *(Copyright Don Powell)* **Bottom Right** - The amount of tomato puree used by the CWS at Lowestoft was considerable. At the No. 1 factory, Peter Harvey is seen moving a pallet holding four tomato puree containers using a fork lift. *(Copyright Peter Calvert)*

Left - With work associated with the Sauces and Pickles factory and the Ready Meal complex complete, attention was given to tidying up the outside of the property. With the white painted CWS Hall on the left, work is in progress putting the new kerb in place along Riverside Road. **Right** - Once occupied by the railway line, the roadside verge adjacent to the No. 1 factory was grassed and had trees planted to enhance the area. The trees had just been watered during a hot dry spell in July 1989 when this view was recorded.
(Both photographs copyright Don Powell)

The newly completed entrance to the Ready Meal complex in 1989. The new Sauces and Pickles building together with the new Ready Meal complex gave the impression that the CWS at Lowestoft had a long term future. However, new owners in the 1990s had different ideas.
(Copyright Don Powell)

Looking north along Riverside Road after completion of the major expansion plans of the late 1980s and early 1990s. All the buildings seen here have been demolished and the area is now used for a motor vehicle dealership. The road junction with Waveney Drive is now controlled by traffic lights.
(Copyright Don Powell)

The sign outside the entrance to the newly completed Ready Meal complex. The pathway to the entrance is almost complete and the grass has started to grow.
(Copyright Don Powell)

Boiler Fitter Peter Mobbs on the left and Engineering Supervisor John Jullings on the right outside the entrance to the newly completed Ready Meal complex in August 1989.
(Copyright Don Powell)

Top Left - New continuous cookers were installed during March 1989. This view shows the first section of one of the cookers being manoeuvred into place in what was the No. 1 factory long store. Manufactured by FMC FoodTech, these were used in the cooking of tinned products. **Top Right** - The first two sections of one cooker in position and mounted on blocks. **Bottom Left** - The third section of the cooker being manoeuvred into place in the former long store. **Bottom Right** - The installation of the continuous cookers is complete and they are almost ready for use. Installed by the CWS in 1989, within a few years they were recovered for use elsewhere following the closure of the cannery by the new owners. *(All photographs copyright Don Powell)*

Many people may be surprised at the number of "in house" skilled trades required to keep the vast CWS factory premises and the extensive plant and machinery in good order. David White, an Engineering Apprentice, is seen at work in the main workshop during August 1989.
(Copyright Don Powell)

A time capsule was buried during the building work required for the base of a Mitchell cooker in September 1989.
Holding the capsule is fitter's mate Tony Baxter, with the shovel is George Harvey from the Building Department and next to him is fitter Jeff Bullard. It has not been possible to indentify the chap on the far left. The location is the No. 1 factory cannery.
(Copyright Don Powell)

Opened in 1989, the ready meal unit was accommodated in a refurbished part of the No. 1 factory and a new building. These views, recorded just before the opening in July 1989, give an idea of some of the equipment installed there. As with the Sauces and Pickles complex, this was only in CWS ownership for a few years before passing to new owners.

Top Left - The two fully computerised retorts. These advanced compact machines were made by Rotomatronic and had to be lowered through the roof for installation in the ready meal complex.

Top Right - Part of the Ready Meal production line.

Bottom Left - Maintenance fitter Tom Robbins and Engineer Storeman Brian Knights are seen in this view of part of the production line. Tom is on the left and Brian on the right. *(All photographs courtesy Don Powell)*

The Ready Meal complex was opened on 29th September 1989 by the Rt. Hon. John Selwyn Gummer MP, at that time the Minister of Agriculture, Fisheries, Food. This very hygienic facility was equipped with the most modern plant available but would close within 10 years. **Top Left** - Mr. Gummer has just unveiled the plaque marking the opening of this new important venture for Lowestoft. **Top Right** - Observing a stage in the production of one of the types of ready meal. **Bottom Left** - Sampling the various types of meals produced in the complex. **Bottom Right** - The production of meals continued whilst Mr. Gummer and the opening party inspected the facilities.
(All photographs copyright Neil Watson)

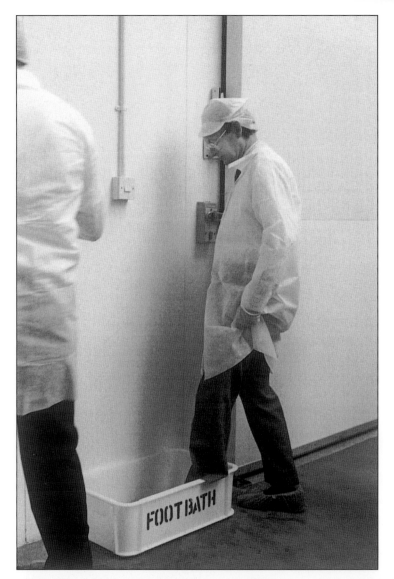

Left - The highest standards of hygiene applied in the ready meal production area as demonstrated here with Mr. Gummer wearing over-shoes and using the foot bath on entry. **Right** - Mr. Gummer inspecting ready meals that are packaged and ready to leave the factory for customers. These particular meals were produced for the Quick Thinking brand. *(Both photographs copyright Neil Watson)*

These two views show the viner shop which was situated close to Lake Lothing. After the viners were no longer maintained by the CWS, a new use was found for the building and a 9000 gallon tank and chlorination system were installed there.

Top - The east end of the building with the very distinctive and well known sign advertising "Waveney" products. Alan Ife is on the left, climbing the ladder.

Bottom - A view showing the west end of the building and looking east across a busy harbour scene that includes Richards shipyard, the Sizewell crane, and offshore standby vessels.

(Both photographs copyright Don Powell)

Maintenance fitter Don Powell is seen making a gear wheel in brass on a Browne & Sharpe milling machine in the No. 2 Factory workshop during September 1989. This machine was made in Providence, Rhode Island, USA. *(Copyright Don Powell)*

Supervisor Albert Norberry retired in January 1990 and is seen here surrounded by many of his work colleagues during the presentation of his retirement gifts. On the far left is Cannery Supervisor Frank Parker. *(Copyright Don Powell)*

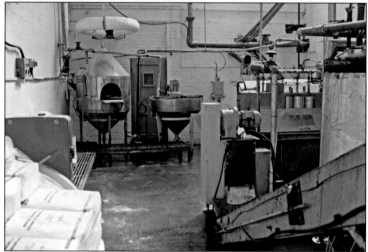

Top Left - By May 1990 construction of the Sauces and Pickles building was well advanced. This view of the south side of the building looking west shows on the extreme left the row of former CWS terrace houses. These fine, robust quality built properties were demolished as part of the site clearance. The public were told at the time the site would be used to create a new business park creating up to 450 jobs. **Top Right** - Another view of the south side of the building during construction but looking east. Following the closure of the Sauces and Pickles plant in 1997, the building was not demolished and is now home to a forklift company. Historically, it is important since it remains the only former CWS building at Lowestoft to survive in the 21st century. **Bottom Left** - Surrounded by farewell gifts and work colleagues, Albert Besford is seen here with Mrs. Besford on his retirement in 1989. Albert worked at the factories as a painter. **Bottom Right** - Part of the Liquor Room in August 1989 showing the can opening plant on the right with three cans visible, the mixing hopper in the corner and bags of corn flour, a thickening agent, on the left. (*All photographs copyright Don Powell*)

Top Left -The north side of the Sauces and Pickles building faced Lake Lothing and looking east, the well known Richards shipyard was a close neighbour. This evening scene recorded in June 1990 shows the tanker *Alacrity* under construction at the shipyard. **Top Right** - Close proximity to Richards meant that the quayside of the No. 1 factory provided superb opportunities to view ships being launched there. The large ferry *Caledonian Isles* is seen here on her launch day ready to enter the water. This very impressive ship, completed in 1993, was the last vessel to be built at this historic shipyard. A large ASDA superstore now occupies the site. **Bottom Left** - A few moments after launching and the *Caledonian Isles* passes close to the factory quayside. The tugs *Trimley* and *Sun Surrey* are ready to take charge of the vessel. These scenes provide a reminder of two of Lowestoft's bygone major industrial concerns, both of which at one time employed hundreds of folk. **Bottom Right** -The CWS owned a long section of quay and for many years this fine three masted vessel, the *Heartsease*, was a resident there. After much restoration, the 1903 built vessel left Lowestoft for the south coast. *(All photographs copyright Don Powell)*

During August 1990 new windows were fitted to the General Office. The large notice board on the extreme right gives details of firms involved in the construction of the new Sauces and Pickles building and advises that this is further expansion by the CWS in Lowestoft.
(Copyright Don Powell)

The Pea Field offices were for many years a notable feature of Riverside Road because of their construction and shed like appearance. They are seen here in July 1990 with the prominent roof of the Ice Company main building behind.
(Copyright Don Powell)

The quayside view looking west from the Sauces and Pickles building. Three CWS employees are taking advantage of this fine location and are enjoying fishing in Lake Lothing on this pleasant sunny day in June 1990.
(Copyright Don Powell)

A general view of No. 1 factory can labelling in December 1990 showing the overhead can tracks.
(Copyright Don Powell)

End of an era at the factories. The Building Department was disbanded in December 1991 and members of that department are seen here in the Carpenters Shop at the time of the disbandment. From left to right are George Harvey, Paul Davies, supervisor John Dunall, Barry Dale, Paul Manthorpe, Jeff Ward, Dick ?, Barry Baldry, the factory plumber David Wicks and Billy Nichols.
(Copyright Don Powell)

Amongst the more traditional farewell presents given to Liquor Room charge hand Charlie Helliwell on his retirement, was a bundle of wire as a memento of his time with the CWS. On the wall behind Charlie and his colleagues can be seen one of the employee clocking-in card racks that existed in the No. 1 factory.
(Copyright Don Powell)

Left - A general view of the pea cleaning plant at the Pea Field in 1991.
Right - An articulated lorry unloading a consignment of peas in 1991 at the No. 1 factory
(Both photographs copyright Don Powell)

Top left - A further scene from 1991 as bulk loads of peas are delivered for processing and canning. Peas were brought to Lowestoft from many destinations and it is possible that these had just arrived from Lincolnshire.
(Copyright Don Powell)

Top Right - After removal of the dirt and debris that had arrived with the peas, they passed into a hopper before being weighed on the scales below. *(Copyright Don Powell)*

Bottom Right - Peas passing through the de-stoner in 1991 prior to being pumped into the cannery.
(Copyright Don Powell)

Top Left - Two ladies working on ready meal production in the Riverside Road complex in late 1989. **Top Right** - With only a few years operational life at Lowestoft before being recovered for use elsewhere, the latest equipment was installed in the No. 1 factory. This is the Doboy shrink wrap plant in operation, placing and wrapping cans onto trays ready for despatch to stores across the UK. **Bottom Left** - A scene in the No. 1 factory of a Slatband conveyor with cans of marrowfat peas approaching the Doboy shrink wrap plant prior to being palletised. **Bottom Right** - On 9th December 1991, the Lowestoft factories manager received the British Standards Institute "Certificate of Registration of Assessed Capability" from the then local MP, Mr. David Porter. The award covered many aspects of food processing at the Lowestoft factories. (*All photographs copyright Neil Watson*)

Top Left - In 1994, ownership of the CWS subsidiary F.E. Barber passed to Hobson plc and consequently all the familiar CO-OP signs were removed from the premises. The illuminated sign above the office entrance at the No. 2 factory was removed on 28th May 1994. **Top Right** - The sign is gently lowered to the ground allowing the lighting units normally hidden behind the panel to be seen. A prominent feature of Waveney Drive for many years, the sign would have made a worthy exhibit in a local museum, but that was not to be. No significant reminders of the original factories remain, in fact there is little to show the factories ever existed. **Bottom Left** - The sign on the ground with the three CWS employees given the task of removing it . On the left is Paul Davies, in the centre Paul Fuller and on the right Norman Rodwell. **Bottom Right** - Other CO-OP signs removed from the factory premises included that on the Stork Cooker tower. The date is the 28th May 1994. *(All photographs copyright Don Powell)*

After removal of the Perspex panel sign, the backing board was removed.
Left - The view from just inside the No. 1 factory gate. **Right** - Removal of the board using the fork lift truck.
(Both photographs copyright Don Powell)

Top Left - A similar task of removing signs had been carried out the previous day at the Sauces and Pickles building in Riverside Road. Undertaking the task there is Norman Rodwell on the left and Monty Blake on the right. **Top Right** - During 1995, recovery of equipment was a common sight throughout the No. 1 factory. This particular scene shows the soup room with equipment being dismantled. **Bottom Left** - After the closure of the cannery the FMC continuous cookers were destined for further use at a different location. Alan Ife and Kenny Schofield are seen here jacking up a cooker ready for recovery. A pile of recovered metal work can be seen in the background on the floor. **Bottom Right** - A sad scene in August 1995 inside what had been Can Labelling in the No. 1 factory. All the plant and lines have been recovered and the building awaits an uncertain future. This turned out to be demolition. *(All photographs copyright Don Powell)*

To find any reminders of the vast CWS Lowestoft estate is now virtually impossible and this large CO-OP sign would have made an ideal exhibit in a local museum. Instead it finished up in a skip for scrap materials after being taken down with the change of ownership. *(Copyright Don Powell)*

The Christmas greetings cards on the back wall and the mince pies on the table create a seasonal atmosphere in the electricians workshop. The date is 23rd December 1994 and enjoying their break are from left to right:- Monty Blake, Peter Mobbs, Paul Rose, Tony Banthorpe, Neil Andrews, Kevin Blowers, and Norman Rodwell.
Although some are wearing work clothes with the CO-OP logo on, the factory was no longer owned by the CWS.
(Copyright Don Powell)

Together with the factory clock, the office entrance doorway in the No. 2 factory was a well known and much admired feature of Waveney Drive. Many official photographs used this doorway as a backdrop. With only a short while left before being destroyed with the demolition of the factory, it still retained an air of grandeur. The remaining brass plate to the left of the door gives F. E. Barber Ltd., Hanover Street, Manchester 4, as the registered owner of the property. By then, Hobson plc owned F. E. Barber Ltd. with Hillsdown Holdings later becoming involved through ownership of Hobson plc.
(Copyright Malcolm White)

During the life of the factories, the CWS Hall was used for a great many purposes and continued in use for such events as a community diners club, and car boot and jumble sales after the factories closed. Here we see the Hall shortly before it was demolished. The land immediately in front of the building was once occupied by a railway siding.
(Copyright Malcolm White)

The Stork Cooker tower was a prominent feature of the No. 1 factory and a superb vantage point to record scenes of the harbour area that are now becoming distant memories. The once important shipyard seen here is now the location of the ASDA superstore and the two ships seen on the right of the top photograph and on the left in the bottom photograph are the *Cirolana* and *Corystes,* at one time Lowestoft based research vessels. *(Copyright Peter Calvert)*

Two further views recorded from the Stork Cooker Tower with a view of the former shipyard in the top photograph and looking across Kirkley in the bottom photograph. *(Copyright Peter Calvert)*

Within a few weeks of this scene being recorded, the No. 1 factory building would be no more. This November 1998 view shows the scaffolding contractor at work erecting scaffolding to allow removal of a section of roof.
(Copyright Malcolm White)

This view of the No. 1 factory was also recorded in November 1998 and shows the very noticeable overhead structure over Riverside Road carrying services between the two factories.
(Copyright Malcolm White)

Top Left - Demolition of the No. 1 factory; soon a Japanese car dealership would occupy this location. *(Copyright Malcolm White)* **Top Right** - Amongst all the destruction the former CWS Sauces and Pickles factory seen here in the ownership of Barber Richmore, was untouched and the building survives today. *(Copyright Stanley Earl)* **Bottom Left** - The No. 2 factory building appears defiant in the face of demolition, however within days this sturdy brick building would be reduced to heaps of rubble. This view was recorded from Waveney Drive in February 2000. *(Copyright Don Powell)* **Bottom Right** - The public were told that following the demolition of the No. 2 factory a business park would be established there. This was subsequently changed. Another view from February 2000 of the demolition of this substantial and well maintained building. *(Copyright Don Powell)*

Top Left - The No. 2 factory building a few years before demolition as seen from Kimberley Road. *(Copyright Stanley Earl)* **Top Right** - An unusual view of the north side of the No. 1 factory a few years before demolition. *(Copyright Stanley Earl)* **Bottom Left** - What German bombs in World War Two failed to do, the demolition contractor soon achieved as the No. 2 factory rapidly disappears. *(Copyright Stanley Earl)* **Bottom Right** - Sunset over the remains of the No. 2 factory. *(Copyright Don Powell)*

One of the final acts in the demolition of the No. 2 factory was when the chimney received the attention of the demolition contractor. Soon this great landmark would just be a memory as it joined many other historic features, buildings and streets of Lowestoft that have been removed to make way for redevelopment and regeneration. *(Both photographs copyright Neil Watson)*

The CWS Retired Employees Association meets regularly in the hall at the United Reformed Church in Lowestoft. These scenes were recorded at their Christmas 2003 meeting and show the members playing bingo and enjoying the buffet.
(All photographs copyright Don Powell)

Maconochie Bros. Memorabilia (1)

The Lowestoft factories were built by Maconochie's and later purchased by the CWS. With their established presence in Great Yarmouth, it is doubtful whether the CWS would ever had come to Lowestoft had it not been for the Maconochie factories being available. A dispute with the local council appears to have been the main reason for the Maconochie departure from Lowestoft.

A selection of labels from Maconochie Bros. products:-
Above - A label from a can of the famous Army Ration Beef and Vegetable stew**.**
Below - On the **left** is a label from a jar of Red Cabbage, it is believed this was a Lowestoft product. In the **centre** is a Black Pepper label dating from 1916 and on the **right** is a label from a jar of Chambers Pickles. This is reputed to have been produced at the Maconochie Lowestoft factory around 1905.
Please note that these labels have been reduced in size for use in this publication use and are not to scale. The originals date from the period 1905-20. *(The Malcolm White Collection)*

Maconochie Bros. Memorabilia (2)

What became the CWS No. I factory produced a wide range of food products whilst in the ownership of the Maconochie Bros. and although difficult to prove, it is likely that some of the products on this and the previous page would have been Lowestoft produced. The CWS, with both factories in production, increased the range of food products made at Lowestoft substantially. As is the case with the labels on the previous page, those seen here are reduced in size and are not to scale.

Above - Further Maconochie Bros. food product labels. The Plum Jam and Army Ration Stew date from 1905-20 and the Herring Cutlets from the 1920s-30s. *(The Malcolm White Collection)*

Below - These advertisements are for two Manonochie products, "Kep" sauce and "Pan Yan" pickle. Both were introduced when the company was making food products in Lowestoft. *(The Malcolm White Collection)*

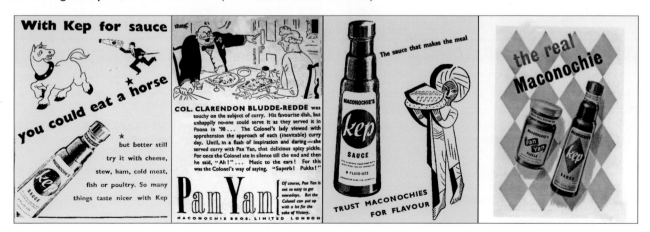

CWS Memorabilia - Original Admission Ticket to the Great Co-operative Exhibition

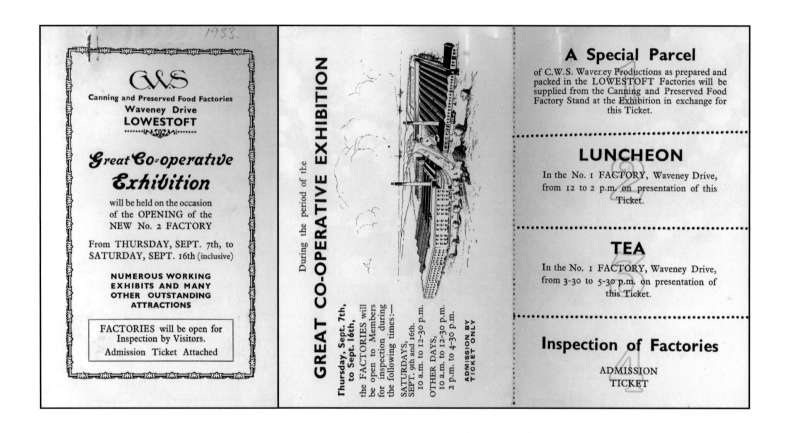

The impressive building later known as the No. 2 factory was acquired by the CWS in 1932 and the Great Co-operative Exhibition was held at Lowestoft in September 1933 on the occasion of the official opening of this factory. During the period between the purchase and opening of the building it had been altered and equipped to suit the requirements of the new owner and had seen some limited production. This admission ticket to the Exhibition is a reduced size copy of an intact original which is in the author's collection. The four coupons on the third part of the ticket were intended to be torn off and used in exchange for a free parcel of Lowestoft CWS food products, a free luncheon and tea and also admission to the factories. It is fortunate that this particular ticket was never used and still exists in almost mint condition thereby allowing us to sample the community spirit generated by the CWS and the pride they had in their Lowestoft operation.
(Copyright Co-operative (CWS) Group Ltd./The Malcolm White Collection)

CWS Memorabilia - Original Lowestoft Advertising Card

This very rare and finely detailed innovative card was issued by the CWS to illustrate their major investment in Lowestoft and the success of their large canning and food processing factories there. The CWS estate at Lowestoft was large and this 1930s promotional advertising card shows not only the size of the factories but also gives some interesting sales figures that show a significant increase after the purchase and bringing into production of the former Maconochie Bros. second factory which became the CWS No. 2 factory.

The card is shown here as a much reduced copy of the original which is in the author's collection. A great deal of detail has been incorporated in the drawing of the estate and includes the CWS factory railway sidings complete with a train about to leave loaded with CWS products, both factory chimneys, ships in the Inner Harbour with one at the CWS quay, the sports field, CWS cottages, CWS hall, attractive tree lined roadways, open countryside, early motor vehicles in Waveney Drive, Riverside Road and the loading area of the No. 1 factory. In addition to the Lowestoft factories sales figures, the clever variations of the CWS theme by the card designers should be noted. The Lowestoft factories were considered very modern with the No. 2 factory relatively new in the 1930s and this has been noted by those responsible for the messages on the cards. As has been already expressed elsewhere in this book, after purchase by regeneration agents and developers, the factories and the estate were erased from the landscape and the site cleared ready to be used for other purposes. Early maps of this area indicate that much of the CWS estate was at one time marshland. *(Copyright Co-operative (CWS) Group Ltd./The Malcolm White Collection)*

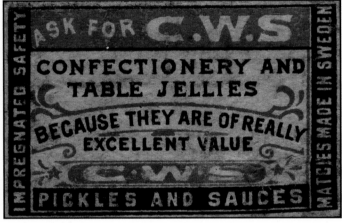

Further examples of advertisements promoting Lowestoft made or related products.

Left - From the publication "The CWS Motorists & Cyclists Compendium of England & Wales", this advertisement illustrates many of the savory delights made in Lowestoft.
Right - The CWS used a variety of methods to advertise their products including matchbox labels. This label has been enlarged for use in this book.
(Copyright Co-operative (CWS) Group Ltd./The Malcolm White Collection)

These advertisements are from the publication "The CWS Book of Party Games". This was a popular book containing instructions and full colour illustrations of 39 games to play at Christmas and other times whenever a group of family or friends were gathered together. The games included the Balloon Game, Birds of the Air, Blindfold Feeding, Bogie, Changing Hats, Charades, Coded Messages, Confessions, Danger Zone, Forfeits, Pokey, Power of Observation, Thus and So, Spinning the Plate, Spotting the Change, Treasure Hunt and Underground. At the time the book was published, a high proportion of the British population were members of retail co-operative societies and families tended to be larger than today. The use of the book declined in popularity after the widespread introduction of television and later, computers in the home. The aim of the book was partly to increase the sales of CWS products that were suitable for use at parties such as potato crisps together with potted meat and cheese spread sandwiches that often included beetroot, all of which were produced at Lowestoft. The extensive Bakery in the No. 2 factory used large amounts of CWS Flour to produce a fine range of pies suitable for party fare. *(Copyright Co-operative (CWS) Group Ltd./The Malcolm White Collection)*

CWS Memorabilia - Gift Request Form and 1947 Social Programme

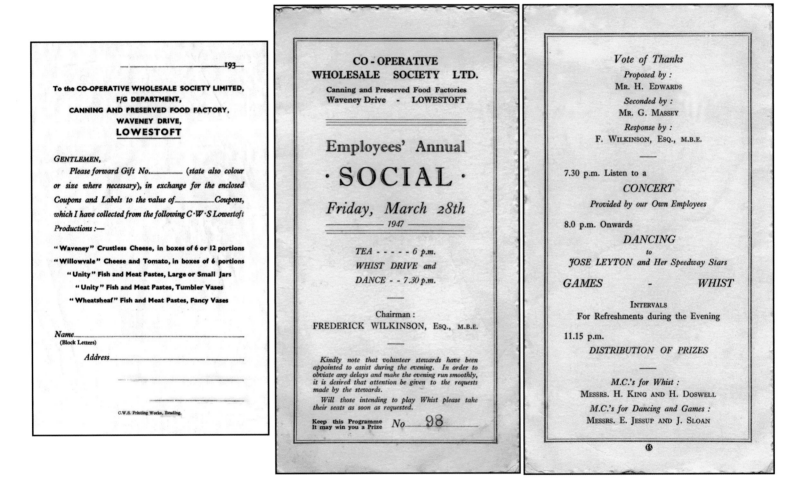

---193----

To the CO-OPERATIVE WHOLESALE SOCIETY LIMITED,
F/G DEPARTMENT,
CANNING AND PRESERVED FOOD FACTORY,
WAVENEY DRIVE,
LOWESTOFT

GENTLEMEN,

Please forward Gift No............... (state also colour or size where necessary), in exchange for the enclosed Coupons and Labels to the value of..................Coupons, which I have collected from the following C·W·S Lowestoft Productions :—

"Waveney" Crustless Cheese, in boxes of 6 or 12 portions
"Willowvale" Cheese and Tomato, in boxes of 6 portions
"Unity" Fish and Meat Pastes, Large or Small Jars
"Unity" Fish and Meat Pastes, Tumbler Vases
"Wheatsheaf" Fish and Meat Pastes, Fancy Vases

Name..................
(Block Letters)
Address..................

C.W.S. Printing Works, Reading.

CO - OPERATIVE
WHOLESALE SOCIETY LTD.

Canning and Preserved Food Factories
Waveney Drive - LOWESTOFT

Employees' Annual
· SOCIAL ·

Friday, March 28th
------ 1947 ------

TEA - - - - - 6 p.m.

WHIST DRIVE and

DANCE - - 7.30 p.m.

Chairman :
FREDERICK WILKINSON, Esq., M.B.E.

Kindly note that volunteer stewards have been appointed to assist during the evening. In order to obviate any delays and make the evening run smoothly, it is desired that attention be given to the requests made by the stewards.

Will those intending to play Whist please take their seats as soon as requested.

Keep this Programme No 98
It may win you a Prize

Vote of Thanks
Proposed by :
MR. H. EDWARDS
Seconded by :
MR. G. MASSEY
Response by :
F. WILKINSON, ESQ., M.B.E.

7.30 p.m. Listen to a
CONCERT
Provided by our Own Employees

8.0 p.m. Onwards
DANCING
to
JOSE LEYTON and Her Speedway Stars

GAMES - WHIST

INTERVALS
For Refreshments during the Evening

11.15 p.m.
DISTRIBUTION OF PRIZES

M.C.'s for Whist :
MESSRS. H. KING AND H. DOSWELL

M.C.'s for Dancing and Games :
MESSRS. E. JESSUP AND J. SLOAN

Above Left - A copy of a request form for a gift under the vouchers for gifts and labels scheme administered from the Lowestoft No. 2 factory. The vouchers and labels were available with CWS products and could be exchanged for gifts detailed in a catalogue.
(Copyright Co-operative (CWS) Group Ltd./The Peter Killby Collection)

Above Centre and Right - The 1947 Annual Employees Social was held in the CWS Hall in Riverside Road and the evening's events can be seen in this copy of the programme. A comprehensive range of entertainment was arranged for those attending.
(Copyright Co-operative (CWS) Group Ltd./The Mabel Haylock Collection)

CWS Memorabilia - Original Factory Advertisements from the period 1940-1960

Both these advertisements were used in nationwide publicity campaigns, thus ensuring that the factories and the town were well known across the British Isles. The CWS actively encouraged members and others to visit the factories, which were one of the main food production centres in the country producing a wide range of goods.

(Copyright Co-operative (CWS) Group Ltd./The Peter Killby Collection)

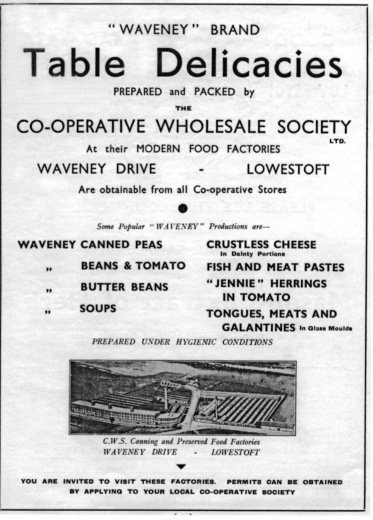

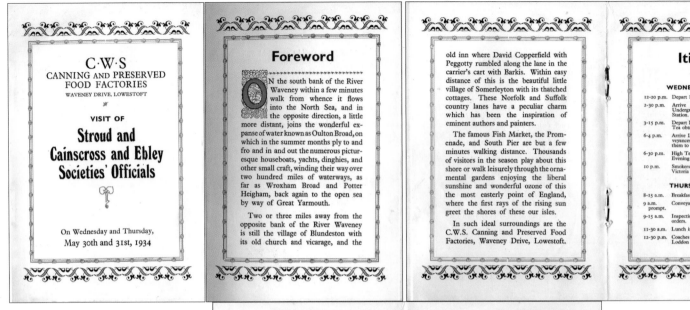

C·W·S
CANNING AND PRESERVED
FOOD FACTORIES
WAVENEY DRIVE, LOWESTOFT

VISIT OF

Stroud and
Cainscross and Ebley
Societies' Officials

On Wednesday and Thursday,
May 30th and 31st, 1934

Foreword

ON the south bank of the River Waveney within a few minutes walk from whence it flows into the North Sea, and in the opposite direction, a little more distant, joins the wonderful expanse of water known as Oulton Broad, on which in the summer months ply to and fro and in and out the numerous picturesque houseboats, yachts, dinghies, and other small craft, winding their way over two hundred miles of waterways, as far as Wroxham Broad and Potter Heigham, back again to the open sea by way of Great Yarmouth.

Two or three miles away from the opposite bank of the River Waveney is still the village of Blundeston with its old church and vicarage, and the old inn where David Copperfield with Peggotty rumbled along the lane in the carrier's cart with Barkis. Within easy distance of this is the beautiful little village of Somerleyton with its thatched cottages. These Norfolk and Suffolk country lanes have a peculiar charm which has been the inspiration of eminent authors and painters.

The famous Fish Market, the Promenade, and South Pier are but a few minutes walking distance. Thousands of visitors in the season play about this shore or walk leisurely through the ornamental gardens enjoying the liberal sunshine and wonderful ozone of this the most easterly point of England, where the first rays of the rising sun greet the shores of these our isles.

In such ideal surroundings are the C.W.S. Canning and Preserved Food Factories, Waveney Drive, Lowestoft.

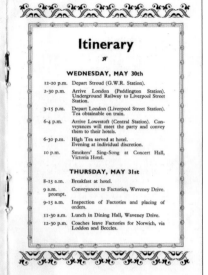

Itinerary

WEDNESDAY, MAY 30th

12-30 p.m.	Depart Stroud (G.W.R. Station).
2-30 p.m.	Arrive London (Paddington Station). Underground Railway to Liverpool Street Station.
3-15 p.m.	Depart London (Liverpool Street Station). Tea obtainable on train.
6-4 p.m.	Arrive Lowestoft (Central Station). Conveyances will meet the party and convey them to their hotels.
6-30 p.m.	High Tea served at hotel. Evening at individual discretion.
10 p.m.	Smokers' Sing-Song at Concert Hall, Victoria Hotel.

THURSDAY, MAY 31st

8-15 a.m.	Breakfast at hotel.
9 a.m. prompt.	Conveyances to Factories, Waveney Drive.
9-15 a.m.	Inspection of Factories and placing of orders.
11-30 a.m.	Lunch in Dining Hall, Waveney Drive.
12-30 p.m.	Coaches leave Factories for Norwich, via Loddon and Beccles.

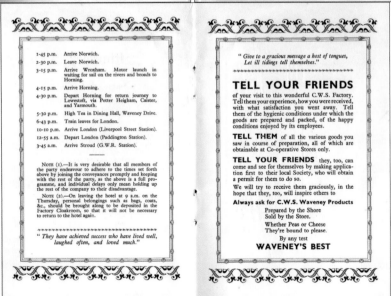

1-45 p.m.	Arrive Norwich.
2-30 p.m.	Leave Norwich.
3-15 p.m.	Arrive Wroxham. Motor launch in waiting for sail on the rivers and broads to Horning.
4-15 p.m.	Arrive Horning.
4-30 p.m.	Depart Horning for return journey to Lowestoft, via Potter Heigham, Caister, and Yarmouth.
5-30 p.m.	High Tea in Dining Hall, Waveney Drive.
6-43 p.m.	Train leaves for London.
10-10 p.m.	Arrive London (Liverpool Street Station).
12-55 a.m.	Depart London (Paddington Station).
3-45 a.m.	Arrive Stroud (G.W.R. Station).

NOTE (1).—It is very desirable that all members of the party endeavour to adhere to the times set forth above by joining the conveyances promptly and keeping with the rest of the party, as the above is a full programme, and individual delays only mean holding up the rest of the company to their disadvantage.

NOTE (2).—On leaving the hotel at 9 a.m. on the Thursday, personal belongings such as bags, coats, &c., should be brought along to be deposited in the Factory Cloakroom, so that it will not be necessary to return to the hotel again.

" They have achieved success who have lived well, laughed often, and loved much."

" Give to a gracious message a host of tongues, Let ill tidings tell themselves."

TELL YOUR FRIENDS

of your visit to this wonderful C.W.S. Factory. Tell them your experience, how you were received, with what satisfaction you went away. Tell them of the hygienic conditions under which the goods are prepared and packed, of the happy conditions enjoyed by its employees.

TELL THEM of all the various goods you saw in course of preparation, all of which are obtainable at Co-operative Stores only.

TELL YOUR FRIENDS they, too, can come and see for themselves by making application first to their local Society, who will obtain a permit for them to do so.

We will try to receive them graciously, in the hope that they, too, will inspire others to

Always ask for C.W.S. Waveney Products

Prepared by the Shore
Sold by the Store.

Whether Peas or Cheese
They're bound to please.

By any test
WAVENEY'S BEST

A typical programme for a visit to the factories by a co-operative society. This is reduced in size for inclusion in this book and it should be noted that reference to the River Waveney refers to Lake Lothing. *(Copyright Co-operative (CWS) Group Ltd./The Malcolm White Collection)*

CWS Memorabilia - Original Factory Advertisements from the period 1940-1960

"Waveney" Brand Table Delicacies

PREPARED and PACKED by

THE CO-OPERATIVE WHOLESALE SOCIETY LTD.,

At their MODERN FOOD FACTORIES,

WAVENEY DRIVE   -   LOWESTOFT.

Are obtainable from all Co-operative Stores.

Some Popular "WAVENEY" Productions are

WAVENEY CANNED PEAS	CRUSTLESS CHEESE In dainty portions
" BEANS & TOMATO	FISH & MEAT PASTES
" BUTTER BEANS	"JENNIE" HERRINGS IN TOMATO
" SOUPS	TONGUES, MEATS & GALANTINES in glass moulds

Prepared Under Hygienic Conditions.

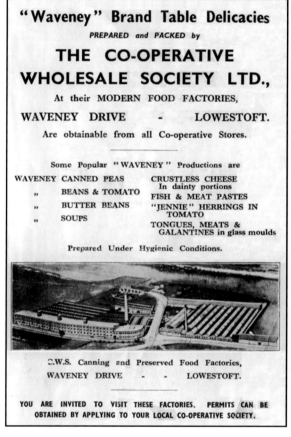

C.W.S. Canning and Preserved Food Factories,
WAVENEY DRIVE   -   -   LOWESTOFT.

YOU ARE INVITED TO VISIT THESE FACTORIES. PERMITS CAN BE OBTAINED BY APPLYING TO YOUR LOCAL CO-OPERATIVE SOCIETY.

LOOK TO LOWESTOFT FOR FINE FOODS

From delightful Lowestoft, the joy of holiday-makers, come delicious WAVENEY foods, the joy of all who love good things to eat. Prepared and packed by one of the most hygienic and up-to-the-minute plants in the country, WAVENEY foods offer a wide choice of tasty varieties. Ask your Co-operative Society to arrange a visit to the WAVENEY factories. We shall be delighted to show you round.

WAVENEY

THE BEST IN PRESERVED FOODS

FROM CO-OPERATIVE STORES

Some WAVENEY favourites

Canned Garden Peas . Canned Soups
Canned Carrots . Fish and Meat Pastes
Canned Processed Peas . Canned Herrings in
Tomato Sauce . Canned Beans in Tomato Sauce
Canned Sweet Puddings . Canned Spaghetti in
Tomato with Cheese Sauce . Waveney
Processed Cheese . Willow Vale Cheese Spread

---

you are invited to...

Look for the "Waveney Mark"—it's a sign that in the can there's JUST HONEST-TO-GOODNESS GOODNESS

COME AND SEE US !

Visitors to our factory are welcomed

Ask for

Fish and Meat Pastes
Canned Processed Peas
Beans in Tomato Sauce
Canned Soups
Canned Sweet Puddings
"Jennie" Herrings in Tomato
Canned Beetroot
Spaghetti in Tomato Sauce, with cheese
Canned Carrots
Canned Garden Peas

try C·W·S canned foods

INVITATION

We of the famous WAVENEY factory of the C.W.S offer a warm and sincere welcome to all who would like to look around and see for themselves how C.W.S CANNED FOODS are made.

Ask your CO-OPERATIVE SOCIETY to arrange a visit for you and your friends.

MADE AND PACKED BY THE C.W.S AT
WAVENEY DRIVE, LOWESTOFT, AND OBTAINABLE *from your Co-operative Society*

Further advertisements publicising the CWS Lowestoft factories. At the time these advertisements appeared in the 1950s, CWS sales were in the order of £444,285,000 per annum of which food sales were £311,915,000. A large proportion of the food sales were products from the Lowestoft factories. The 1957 combined membership of the 757 retail co-operative societies, 85 federal societies and 98 agricultural societies in England, Northern Ireland and Wales was 11,750,000. There were 31,000 retail shops plus thousands of bread, coal and milk roundsmen serving the community. (Copyright Co-operative (CWS) Group Ltd./The Malcolm White Collection)

PHOTOGRAPHIC INDEX

Please note groups are in alphabetical order except the employees section which is in surname order.

1995

2000

2007
(All Photographs copyright Mike Page)